Women, Education, and Politics

'*Sufi Ke Adarsho Per Yakin Rakhne Wale Jin Buzoorgo Ne Ye Idara Qayam Kiya Tha Ye College Un Adarsho Ka Muhafiz Aur Ayanadar Tha... Talibat Hindustan Ke Mukhtalif Hisse Se Aye Thi Aur Har Firqa Se Taluq Rakhti Thi, Yeh Ek Khushbash Mushtarka Khandan Tha*'

('Believers of Sufi principles and ideals, such elderly [respectable] men had established this institution, this college was the protector and mirror of these principles...The students came from different parts of Hindustan and were in contact with every group and section [of the people], this [college] was a happy, joint family.')

—Qurratullain Haider (former student of the college, 1941–45)

'IP always believed in high ideals and we were taught never to compromise on this score... Dedicated teachers were on hand to guide—but not curb our youthful spirits. And simplicity of dress coupled with a modern mental outlook were the mark of our traditions.'

—Padma Shri Sharan Rani Backliwal (former student of the college in the early 1950s)

Women, Education, and Politics

The Women's Movement and Delhi's Indraprastha College

Meena Bhargava
and
Kalyani Dutta

OXFORD
UNIVERSITY PRESS

OXFORD
UNIVERSITY PRESS

YMCA Library Building, Jai Singh Road, New Delhi 110 001

Oxford University Press is a department of the University of Oxford. It furthers
the University's objective of excellence in research, scholarship, and education
by publishing worldwide in

Oxford   New York

Auckland   Cape Town   Dar es Salaam   Hong Kong   Karachi   Kuala Lumpur
Madrid   Melbourne   Mexico City   Nairobi   New Delhi   Shanghai
Taipei   Toronto

With offices in

Argentina   Austria   Brazil   Chile   Czech Republic   France   Greece   Guatemala
Hungary   Italy   Japan   Poland   Portugal   South Korea   Singapore   Switzerland
Thailand   Turkey   Ukraine   Vietnam

Oxford is a registered trade mark of Oxford University Press
in the UK and in certain other countries

Published in India
By Oxford University Press, New Delhi

© Oxford University Press, 2005

ISBN   0 19 566911 8

Typeset in Gatineau 10/12 by R. K. Computers, Delhi 110 051
Printed at Rashtriya Printers, New Delhi 110 032
Plished by Manzar Khan, Oxford University Press
YMCA Library Building, Jai Singh Road, New Delhi 110 001

Contents

PLATES   (between pages 72 and 73)

Acknowledgements

This book commemorates the struggles and triumphs of women's education in India. It is a story of philanthropists and reformers, who despite several hurdles had stood strong to bring education to women. To understand and appreciate the social consciousness and social responsibility of these men and women, we weave our narrative around Indraprastha College of Delhi University, one of the pioneers of women's education in north India.

We owe this book to many. Dr Aruna Sitesh, the Principal of Indraprastha College was a constant source of inspiration and encouragement. We will always remember the indulgence and affection of Dr Sheila UttamSingh, the former Principal of the college. It is unfortunate that despite her deep interest in this work, she could not see it in print.

We are grateful to the two members of the governing body, Shri Narain Prasad and Shri BrijBans Kishore for their invaluable support in providing us the material on the college. Shri Narain Prasad's *haveli* in Chandni Chowk served as the Archives for several months of our data collection. We could not have accessed the exhaustive material on the college without the generosity and help of Mrs Madhu Gupta, the Personal Secretary of Shri Narain Prasad and also an alumna of the college. Shri BrijBans Kishore provided us important files and books on the college. We are deeply indebted to those alumnae of the college, who agreed to share their experiences or be interviewed, notwithstanding their frail health. They appear on several occasions in the pages of this book.

We acknowledge with gratitude the assistance rendered by the staff of Indraprastha College Library, National Archives of India, Nehru Memorial Museum and Library, All India Women's Conference, Centre for Women Development Studies and Sahitya Akademi in New Delhi.

Even as this book celebrates women's education and women empowerment, it felicitates over 75 years of achievement of Indraprastha College. It is to Indraprastha College and its students that we dedicate this book.

New Delhi

Meena Bhargava
Kalyani Dutta

Introduction

This work ventures into studying trends of women's education and women's role in national politics in India. To understand the development of education for Indian women we concentrate primarily on the twentieth century—a period when education for women was not unknown but was still shrouded in prejudice. The study of the movement for women's education in India and their participation in politics is attempted primarily through a case study of Delhi's Indraprastha College. Established in 1924, it was the first women's college in Delhi, and, since that time, has fully lived up to its educational commitment, producing confident and independent, liberal and socially conscious women. The evolution and growth in women's education, the transition and change in the status of women, their responses and reactions to national events, and the growth of their self-confidence—these are some of the items of debate and focus in this book.

INDIGENOUS EDUCATION IN PRE-COLONIAL INDIA

Education is an instrument of *fiqr* (rationality), *ziqar* (thought and observation), *ijtihad* (critique and forming of independent opinions), and above all social transformation and economic advancement. It is one of the major factors that can influence and condition people's outlook and aspirations, challenge inequalities in society and preserve an egalitarian order. These benefits of education were however, denied to many in India since antiquity, creating two classes: privileged and underprivileged.[1] The inequality demonstrated itself in a variety of ways—gender, caste, religion, economic status. But whatever the prejudices, they could not obliterate the right to education of the lower orders of *varnashramadharma* and women. In several parts of pre-colonial India, education was not confined to the Brahmins and Kshatriyas alone. It was extended to Muslims and to the Sudras, and other castes as well. And, despite the gender bias that dominated Indian society till the late nineteenth century, women in some parts of the country were educated within the confines of their homes. And in a few regions women went to school breaking the shackles of ignorance and tradition and heralding formal institutional education for women.[2]

Pre-colonial India had a deeply rooted and widespread system of indigenous education, which consisted of a vast network of elementary village schools as well as schools of higher learning. Both Hindus and Muslims had a tradition of learning and scholarship through their indigenous systems, which involved *tols, pathshalas, makhtabs,* and *madrasas.* A British scholar had stated that 'there is no country where the love of learning had so early an origin or has exercised so lasting and powerful an influence. From the simple poets of the Vedic age to the Bengali philosophers of the present day, there has been an uninterrupted succession of teachers and scholars.'[3] Surveys conducted by the officials of the East India Company suggest that village elementary schools were not communal or based on religious or caste identities although they reflected a gender bias. They were open to all boys provided they could pay the expenses. Though the majority of the pupils were Brahmins and Kshatriyas, Vaishyas and Sudras also sent their boys to school.[4]

As compared to boys, however, institutional education for girls was negligible. Social prejudice and superstition prevented the majority of Indians from sending their daughters to school.[5] Most of the girls who received education did so at home. However, as mentioned above, in some regions, they went to school, though in small numbers. Within the Madras Presidency, in Malabar and Jypore zamindari of Vizagapatnam, large numbers of girls from castes other than Brahmins, Chettri and Vaishya attended school. Some Muslim girls received school education in Trichnopoly and Salem. From amongst the Hindu girls, Sudras and other castes attended school in Masulipatnam, Madura, Tinevelli, and Coimbatore.[6] It is difficult to explain as to why only some girls in some regions went to school. The survey reports of the

Company officials are silent on the issue but the Collectors of these regions have observed that all the girls who went to school were slated to be dancing girls or *devadasis* in temples.[7]

The characteristics of indigenous education show that literacy was 'not very restricted' in pre-colonial India but neither was it completely satisfactory. Such complexities notwithstanding, India could still be placed in Parsons' category of 'advanced intermediate' societies, that is, societies which have full literacy for adult males of upper castes. In other words, in pre-colonial India, literacy was almost universal among men of the Brahmin and Kshatriya castes; it was fairly distributed amongst the Vaishyas; the Sudras and other lower castes had access to institutional education but as compared to the upper castes, the literacy rate amongst them was low.[8]

THE COMPANY'S INTERVENTION IN EDUCATION AND ITS IMPACT

For the first 60 years of its stay in India, the British East India Company—a trading, profit-making organization—showed little interest in the education of Indians. It was aware of the need to improve the education scene in India but was reluctant to interfere with Indian traditions for fear of alienating the local people whose support was necessary if the Company wished to legitimize its power and authority.

The Battle of Plassey was a defining event for British presence in India. After this victory, the British embarked on the process of consolidating its rule in India. From then onwards, it encountered issues that compelled it to define its policy towards education in the country.

The immediate reaction of the Company in Bengal was to support the prevailing system of education. Warren Hastings and his officers patronized oriental learning although there were protests against his scheme in both England and India. In 1781, Hastings established the Calcutta *madrasa* to encourage customary Islamic learning, that is, the study and teaching of Muslim law and related subjects. Jonathan Duncan, the Resident at Banaras, founded Banaras Sanskrit College in 1772 for the study of Hindu Law and Philosophy. Mountstuart Elphinstone, the Commissioner of Deccan, established another college for Hindu learning in Pune. Similar patterns were noticed in Delhi, where schools were started for the children of the zamindars to encourage them to read and write the Persian language. Evidently, the Company was motivated by pragmatic considerations: the need for Indian officers well-versed in Sanskrit, Persian, and Arabic to assist in the administration of law in the courts of the Company, and to win the support of the traditional Hindu and Muslim elite. Practical needs however, were not the only factor. Some like Sir William Jones admired India's cultural heritage and developed a keen personal interest in the learning of Sanskrit and other Indian literature. Inspired by Indian learning and knowledge, they went on to form the Royal Asiatic Society.

These diverse attempts may have initiated the evolution of the Company's educational policy and facilitated the process of churning out clerks, who could be employed cheaply, but they were far from providing the Company with a definite and firm plan on education. The Company still remained uncertain on several issues. Should it encourage western or oriental learning? Should the medium of instruction be English or a classical Indian language or the vernaculars? Should the aim of education be mass education or should it cater only to the elite? To resolve these matters, the Company appointed a General Committee of Public Instructions. The debates continued until the intervention of Lord Macaulay, the law member of the Governor General's Council. Through his Minute of 2 February, 1835, Macaulay limited the problem to a decision on the medium of instruction. Championing the cause of English education, Macaulay dismissed the vernaculars as 'poor and rude' and opposed the continuance of institutions of oriental learning, suggesting that they should be closed since they did not serve 'any useful purpose'.[9] Pondering over the medium of instruction in the centres of higher education financed by the government, Macaulay suggested that the choice was between Sanskrit and Arabic on one hand and English on the other, and decided in favour of the latter, famously observing that a 'single shelf of a good European library was worth the whole native literature of India and Arabia'.[10]

The Company responded promptly to Macaulay's propositions, particularly in Bengal. It decided to focus only on the study of western sciences and literature with English as the medium of instruction in all the schools and colleges of Bengal. In evolving its educational policy, the Company was certainly not motivated by philanthropic reasons. It aimed at gaining legitimacy and strengthening political power and authority by educating a handful of Indians and turning them into loyalists. In other words, the purpose of the colonial system of education, as Bhattacharya argues, was 'a means of the preservation and reproduction of colonial authority not only cognitive authority but also political authority among the natives of the colonized country.'[11] Krishna Kumar, however, presents a different perspective on colonial education. He argues that the view of colonial education as a factory, producing clerks, is theoretically weak and historically untenable. According to him, such a view does not consider the distinctions between the ideas underlying an educational system and its practical purposes. No simple model or statement, he reiterates, can explain the varied effects that colonial education had. Colonial education produced political leaders, professionals, and intellectuals, not just office clerks. It bred colonial values in many but at the same time it turned many others against these values. Kumar observes that while the rejection of colonial education could not be sustained for long, the rejection of colonial rule was sustained. To understand the dichotomy, one cannot ignore the role of colonial education in inspiring the rejection of colonial rule.[12]

Whatever the characteristics and complexities of colonial education, it caused widespread anxiety and apprehensions amongst the Indians. They feared that the exclusive patronage of English education could be a step towards ultimate Anglicization and conversion of the people. Most Indian parents refused to send their children to the 'new schools' or the English medium schools founded by the colonial government. There was anxiety that western education might threaten the distinct cultural identity maintained by different religious communities. Sambuddha Chakrabarty argues that in the violent reactions against learning in nineteenth-century Bengal, particularly learning for women, one of the fears expressed was that western scientific education was spawning 'religionless' men and women.[13]

Towards Women's Education

It was in the midst of extreme defiance that the Company debated its plan towards women's education. Restraint but also conviction that women should be educated marked the colonial policy towards women's education. Company officials such as Mountstuart Elphinstone and Lord Dalhousie argued that the 'diffusion of knowledge' among men and women would end many of the social evils which degraded the condition of women in India.[14] Despite understanding the need for moral and financial support for the spread

of women's education, they still did not guarantee schools for girls.[15]
The Government 'purposely abstained from acting towards its female
subjects as it acted towards male' in the field of education, believing
that a scheme of women's education would be unpopular and 'looked
down upon by the mass with fear and dread whether Hindus or
Muslims'.[16] The apprehensions of the Government were reiterated
by William Adam[17] in his report in which he pointed out that a majority
of Hindu women and men believed that if a girl was taught to read
and write she would become a widow soon after marriage. Muslims
shared the prejudices of the Hindus against the education of women.
Adam observed that 'the eastern ideal of female life was one of strict
purity, seclusion and quiet domestic duty and the literature of the
classical languages of India was far too corrupt according to this
ideal to allow of any teaching of it.'[18] The Government believed that
Indians would rise against any attempt 'to submit their women folk
to the equalizing and emancipating influence of instruction'.[19] For
these reasons, the Company initially remained aloof from the issue
of women's education. This is evident from the fact that there is
no reference to the education of Indian women in any of the
general dispatches relating to educational matters submitted to or
received from the Court of Directors during the first half of the
nineteenth century.

When the company did begin to consider the issue of women's
education they had to take several factors, into account. The main
obstacle was the general hostile attitude of Indians towards women's
education and the preference for *zenana* education or education at
home for women. Indian norms and social customs made the British
model of schooling difficult. The insistence in the Indian system was
on a complete segregation of men and women. In such circumstances,
the girls' schools had to be separate institutions employing only women
teachers. Another impediment to women's education was the pre-
puberty marriages of the girls accompanied by burdensome domestic
obligations. Company officials argued that *zenana* lessons were
expensive, cumbersome, and largely ineffective and that schools were
the only practical method of accomplishing women's education. But
before this could be implemented, several questions had to be
answered : What kind of schools? Who would teach? What would be
taught? Which families would send their daughters to school and for
how long? If girls were married early, could they continue their
education after marriage? A consensus on these items was needed

between the Company and the Indian leaders before moral and material support could be provided to women's education.[20]

Even as the Company pondered over ways to facilitate institutional education for women, missionaries and a few Indians made the first efforts in this direction. In 1821, Miss Cooke, deputed by the British and the Foreign School Society, opened a school for girls at Calcutta. By 1826, her endeavours appeared to be rather successful, with 30 schools under her charge, though the number of pupils was a paltry 600. These schools were merged in 1828 into a Central School under a committee called the Ladies Society for Native Female Education. The London and Church Missionary Society founded similar schools.[21] A turning point in the movement for women's education was the establishment of Bethune Girls' School in Calcutta by John Drinkwater Bethune in May 1849. Bethune had succeeded in securing the consent of the Government. By the 1850s, the Government under Lord Dalhousie had begun to take an active interest in the promotion and spread of education amongst girls. More significantly, by supporting J.E.D. Bethune's efforts, Dalhousie put an end to the era of 'official non-interference' and marked the 'beginning of that of open encouragement in the annals of female education in India'.[22]

Continuing the attempts at expanding women's education, in 1882, the Government formed the Indian Education Commission, which made several recommendations for the spread of education amongst women. This policy was reiterated by successive government resolutions. The expansion in women's education was more obvious at the primary level; that at the secondary level was much slower. Higher education of women began even later and there were not more than 50 girls in Arts Colleges in 1891.[23] However, by the turn of the century, the number of girls' schools and the number of students enrolled in them were showing a remarkable rise. By the end of the First World War, there were educational institutions for women in all parts of the country; the enrolment of girls had tripled at the school level and quintupled in the Universities. This increase can be explained by the fact that parents now had more options: they could choose the type of institution, the curriculum, and even the medium of instruction.[24] The parents were no longer hesitant to send their daughters to school provided the new schools could assuage their fears of anglicization, proselytization, and loss of religious faith. In other words, the parents wanted the assurance that the schools would observe Indian customs.[25] Catering to these needs, many of the schools were 'geographically limited, communally bound and caste sensitive'. They were schools for girls only, the teachers were women and the curricula were geared to 'gender-specific socialization'.[26]

WOMEN'S EDUCATION IN DELHI

It was in such circumstances that Indraprastha College took its shape. It began as a school in 1904 amidst strong challenges. First, it debunked the myth of the indispensability of the English language for a 'modern' school by promoting the vernacular language, that is, Hindi as the medium of instruction although English was offered as one of the subjects. This was a successful attempt at emphasizing that modern ideas could spread faster and deeper if propagated in the language familiar to the masses. By introducing Hindi as the medium of instruction, the school implemented the demands of nationalist leaders like Dadabhai Naoroji, Sayyid Ahmed Khan, Justice Ranade, Bal Gangadhar Tilak, and Mahatma Gandhi, who were agitating for the wide use of vernacular Indian languages in the educational system. Second and perhaps most importantly, the founders of Indraprastha School were successful in convincing many conservative middle-class and upper-class families that their values and traditions would be preserved even if their daughters stepped out of their homes to study.

Here, it would be pertinent to elaborate on the apprehensions of the traditional Indian elite and upper-middle-class families in the late nineteenth and early twentieth centuries, when the missionary institutions were actively serving the cause of education in India. To understand the fears and suspicions of those times, it would be worthwhile to refer to Michelle Maskiell's book on the history of Kinnaird College in Lahore. Maskiell describes how wary north Indians were about the religious complexion of the institutions in which even their sons studied. She argues that various religious and social reform groups in the Punjabi society wanted English education for their sons without either the Christian bias of the missionaries or the 'Godless' secular bias of the government schools. She further elaborates that the Arya Samaj as well as the Anjuman-i-Himayat-i-Islam were concerned about providing 'safe' English education for men in the late 1880s.[27] The Arya Samaj opened Dayanand Anglo-Vedic (DAV) schools and colleges and the Gurukul at Kangri, where the emphasis was on Sanskrit and Hindu learning. The seminary at Deoband imparted Islamic learning while the Khalsa colleges taught the tenets of Sikhism.[28] If such caution was exercised for men's schools and colleges, it is only to be expected that there would be greater watchfulness regarding schools and colleges for women. The need was for institutions that would subscribe to certain conservative Indian patterns such as providing the girls the security of *purdah* when they attended school or college. It was in such an environment that Indraprastha School and College made its beginning. By 1922, the number of women's colleges in India had risen to 19.[29] Still, there was no such college in Delhi. Indraprastha College was the first women's college to be established in Delhi in 1924.

The uniqueness of this institution lies in a variety of factors. It was infused with the spirit of making education accessible to all women, cutting across castes and communities. The values that were upheld by this college encouraged not only Hindus but also a large number of Muslim families to send their daughters to study. Women of *purdah-nashini* elite were taught in the *zenana* schools in their homes. But the quality of education imparted was not of very high standard. Gail Minault writes that it was difficult to find women teachers and there were no *ustanis* to teach Muslim girls to read the Holy Koran.[30] Convinced by the character of Indraprastha School and College, there was an appreciable increase in the number of Muslim girl students by the 1930s. The significance of Indraprastha College also lies in its active participation and contributions to the national movement and several political and social pursuits to which it has remained committed over the years. For more than 75 years it has not only built and empowered women but has also vividly demonstrated its liberal and radical thinking. Our purpose in choosing Indraprastha College as a case study is twofold: to understand the resistance and the obstacles faced and surmounted by the movement for women's education in India and secondly, the pioneering role of women in national politics.

NOTES AND REFERENCES

1. Sabyasachi Bhattacharya, 'The Contested Terrain of Education', in Sabyasachi Bhattacharya (ed.), *The Contested Terrain: Perspectives on Education in India*, Orient Longman, New Delhi, 1998, p. 4.

2. See Dharampal, *The Beautiful Tree: Indigenous Indian Education in the Eighteenth Century*, Biblia Impex Private Ltd., New Delhi, 1983. Also see, Shaista

Suhrawardy Ikramullah, *From Purdah to Parliament*, Oxford University Press, New Delhi, 2000.

3. F.W. Thomas, *The History and Prospect of British Education in India in 1891*, cf. Suresh Chandra Ghosh, *The History of Education in Modern India, 1757–1998*, Orient Longman, New Delhi, 2000, p. 6.

4. For instance, in western India and Bengal, Hindu and Muslim boys and boys from various castes went to the same school, received the same instruction, and participated in similar sports and extra-curricular activities. In fact, in Gujarat and south Konkan, the intermingling of Hindu and Muslim students was widely prevalent. See, Aparna Basu, *Essays in the History of Indian Education*, Concept Publishing House, New Delhi, 1982, pp. 1, 29, 31.

5. William Adam in his *Report on the State of Education in Bengal, 1835*, suggested the existence of 1,00,000 village schools in Bengal and Bihar around the 1830s. Much before William Adam, Thomas Munro had stated that every village had a school in Madras Presidency (House of Commons Papers, 1812–13, vol. 7, p. 127). Similar statements were made by G.L. Pendergaast (House of Commons Papers, 1831–32, vol. 9, p. 468) and G.W. Leitner (*History of Education in the Punjab since Annexation and in 1882*) for Bombay Presidency and Punjab respectively. See Dharampal, *The Beautiful Tree*.

6. Dharampal, *The Beautiful Tree*, pp. 36–7.

7. Ibid., p. 37.

8. Aparna Basu, *Essays in the History of Indian Education*, p. 34.

9. H. Sharp (ed.), *Selections from Education Records*, Part I, Calcutta, 1781–1839, p. 109.

10. It may be observed that Macaulay had grown up in the midst of Clapham Evangelists and since his younger days had nurtured thoughts of consolidating the British Empire by propagating English law and culture. See Suresh Chandra Ghosh, *The History of Education in Modern India*, p. 31.

11. Sabyasachi Bhattacharya, 'The Contested Terrain of Education', p. 7.

12. Krishna Kumar, *Political Agenda of Education: A Study of Colonialist and Nationalist Ideas*, Sage Publications, New Delhi, 1991, pp. 23–4.

13. Sambuddha Chakrabarty, *Antare Andare*, Stree, Calcutta, 1995, p. 59.

14. Suresh Chandra Ghosh, *The History of Education in Modern India*, p. 68.

15. Geraldine Forbes, *Women in Modern India*, The New Cambridge History of India, IV.2, Cambridge University Press, 1996, p. 40.

16. Suresh Chandra Ghosh, *The History of Education in Modern India*, p. 69.

17. William Adam, a Christian missionary, was appointed by Lord William Bentinck to survey the state of elementary education in India. He submitted three reports between 1835–8 on indigenous Indian education for some of the districts of Bengal and Bihar.

18. J. Long (ed.), *Three Reports on the State of Education in Bengal and Bihar*, Calcutta, 1868, cf. Suresh Chandra Ghosh, *The History of Education in Modern India*, p. 69.

19. Ibid.

20. Geraldine Forbes, *Women in Modern India*, p. 40.

21. Suresh Chandra Ghosh, *The History of Education in Modern India*, p. 69.

22. Ibid., p. 70. Also see Aparna Basu, *Essays in the History of Indian Education*, p. 20.

23. Aparna Basu, *Essays in the History of Indian Education*, p. 20.

24. Geraldine Forbes, *Women in Modern India*, p. 52.

25. Ibid., p. 54.

26. Ibid., p. 60.

27. Michelle Maskiell, *Women Between Cultures: The Lives of Kinnaird College Alumnae in British India*, Syracuse University, USA, 1984, p. 21.

28. Aparna Basu, "National Education in Bengal", in Sabyasachi Bhattacharya (ed.), *The Contested Terrain*, p. 56.

29. Sri Ram Sharma, *Women and Education*, Discovery Publishing House, New Delhi, 1995, p. 170.

30. See Gail Minault, *Secluded Scholars: Women's Education and Muslim Social Reform in Colonial India* (Gender Studies Series), Oxford University Press, New Delhi, 1998.

1

Educate A Girl
Educate A Family, 1904–23

As we trace the growth of women's education in India, it may be pertinent to suggest that women and education were not strangers to each other since the early times. On the contrary, they shared a close relationship. Yet the bonds between the two—women and education—were fixed and decided by the patriarchal Indian order. In the given system, there was no space for the critique of patriarchy or of Hindu social institutions and religious practices. These social norms continued till some women such as Ramabai in the nineteenth century publicly challenged and opted out of the ancestral customary practices. Ramabai launched an attack on brahmanical patriarchy at a time when even the contemporary male reformers had refrained from confronting it.[1]

THE MAKINGS OF WOMEN'S EDUCATION

Institutional education was a rarity for women in pre-colonial India and until the mid-nineteenth century, *zenana* education or domestic instruction was the accepted custom. At home, women were taught to read religious scriptures, read and write the vernacular language although the concentration was on learning home crafts and subjects of domestic and practical utility.[2] These patterns began to change, however gradually, from the mid-nineteenth century with the efforts of Christian missionaries—the pioneers in women's education. They took the initiative in bringing institutional education to women. A few educated Indian men termed 'male intelligentsia' by Gauri Srivastava further extended the endeavours of the missionaries in this direction. Srivastava uses this term to include such Indian men who were educated in the western system—a system that upheld the importance of democratic, liberal, rational and humanitarian principles as explained by Mill, Comte, Spencer and others. Mill had argued for female equality. Comte and Spencer also wrote about the desirability and indispensability of women's equality. These writings had a deep impact on the educated Indian mind.[3]

But while the social reformers of the nineteenth century were considering the need for educating women, they came up against traditions that prohibited women from being 'introduced to bookish learning'. There was also a hesitation to send girls to schools set up by Christian missionaries because of the fear of proselytization and exposure of women to 'harmful western influences'.[4] These apprehensions were, perhaps, nurtured by the statements like that of Dr Thomas Smyth, who in 1855 declared 'we will not conceal the fact, that our own earnest desire is that India were thoroughly Christianized and we regard our female education as an important means towards that end.'[5] These fears were however, temporarily set aside by John Drinkwater Bethune, who founded Bethune Girls' School in Calcutta in 1849 with government aid. His success lay in the assurance that no interference would be permitted with the religion of the girls who joined the school.

Threats or more appropriately fears of conversion disappeared when Indians themselves started opening schools for girls from the 1850s. To mobilize the support of Hindu families for women's education, essays and articles were written in the 1850s to emphasize that women's education was a part of India's tradition, that it was encouraged in the ancient times and that contrary to being harmful, it was beneficial for women to be educated. It was proclaimed in the 1870s that with women's education 'there will be happiness, welfare and civilized manners in social life' and that the country would show a definite improvement. Education would locate women in the 'modern world of the nation'.[6]

To construct a new, modern Indian woman and create a different social space for her, formal education for women was gradually accepted by the middle of the nineteenth century. But this acceptability was conditioned by certain criteria. It was agreed, for instance in

Bengal (a message which spread to all the provinces subsequently) that formal education was a necessary requirement for a *bhadramahila* (respectable woman). But, while she acquired cultural refinement from education, education should not alienate her from home and neither should she become a *memsahib* (a term used for westernized women). Education, in fact, was to inspire in women virtues like orderliness, thrift, cleanliness, a sense of responsibility, hygiene, and the ability to run a home in the new socio-economic conditions. In other words, to garner support for women's education, it was stipulated that education would further sophisticate the femininity and domestic responsibilities of a woman. For a perfect rendering of these obligations, she needed to be exposed to the outside world and that could be provided only by education. It was also urged that to make new ideas accessible to women, they would be taught in their mother tongue rather than in the English language.[7]

A pioneering effort for women's education worth mentioning here is that initiated by Jyotiba Phule and his wife Savitribai. Their efforts were a challenge to the tradition that it was mostly upper-caste men who educated their wives. Phule argued that the failure to educate women had impoverished the Indian society. He believed that education played a big role in understanding social relations. It liberated the subordinated and guided them into new vistas of social perception. For these reasons, he considered education as indispensable for low-caste women as it was for low-caste men. With these convictions, Phule started his first school for low-caste girls in Pune in 1848. As expected, this outraged the orthodoxy, which exerted social pressure on Phule's family. Facing adverse reactions, Phule found it difficult to hire teachers for his school. Savitribai then took up the challenge of teaching the girls herself. This infuriated the orthodoxy even more. They abused Savitribai, a low-caste woman, for her boldness in first empowering herself and then empowering others like her.[8] The furious Brahmins could hardly undermine Phule's determination to make learning accessible to low castes, particularly low-caste women. He disputed the conservative view of banning learning for low-castes and women, which had restricted knowledge and made it an instrument of power.[9]

By 1854, Bombay and Bengal Presidencies had successfully passed social legislation, seeking to establish educational institutions for women. In the Bombay Presidency, by 1854, there were nine schools for girls. It was the Parsi community which first realized the importance of female education in the Bombay Presidency. Cursetjee Nurserwanjee Cama and Sir Jamsetjee Jeejeebhoy founded Bombay's earliest girls' school and D.K. Karve established the first women's University in Bombay in 1896. While such efforts were afoot to educate women and expose them to the outside world, there were some upper-caste Hindu families in the strongly patriarchal society of Maharashtra who taught their daughters, sisters, and wives at home. Ananta Shastri, a Brahmin, educated his daughter Ramabai in the sacred Sanskrit texts. Later the learned Brahmins of Calcutta gave her the titles of Pandita and Saraswati. Anandibai Joshi, initially taught by her husband, Gopalrai Joshi, became the first Indian woman to receive a degree in medicine from the University of Philadelphia, USA. It was, however, not only the upper-caste Hindu families of Bombay who were educating their women. Amongst the Muslims, Badruddin Tyabji was the first in Bombay to send his daughters to a girls' school, set up by the Zenana Bible Medical Mission in 1876. Tyabji's was also the first family to discard *purdah*.[10]

In Bengal, in the second half of the nineteenth century, the spread of formal education among middle-class women was quite remarkable. To illustrate, we take the example of 95 girls' schools in 1863, which had an attendance of 2,500; these figures went up to 2,238 schools in 1890 with a total number of more than 80,000 students. The boost to higher learning and formal learning came when two Bengali women, Chandramukhi Bose and Kadambini Ganguli, took their BA degrees from the University of Calcutta in 1883. The achievements of these two women is particularly noteworthy since it came at a time when even most British Universities did not accept women on their examination rolls. Kadambini Ganguli subsequently went to a medical college and became the first Indian professionally schooled woman doctor.[11] Another victory for educated women came in 1890, when Kadambini Ganguli, the first woman graduate of Calcutta University, addressed the Congress session. In Banaras, Annie Besant established Central Hindu College in 1898, which was later developed as Banaras Hindu University. These are sporadic examples that illustrate the spirit for women's education in India, which continued to flourish as many more schools and colleges were established for women. By the close of the nineteenth century, education for women had acquired a hold in India but the prejudices against it still remained very strong. Young girls who ventured out of their homes for schools and colleges and parents who agreed to educate their daughters were often subjected to social ostracism.

In Delhi, serious efforts were made by the various denominations of missionaries to impart English learning to girls. The Victoria Boarding School for Christian girls was established in 1876. The school that is now known as Gange High School for girls was established by the Baptists in 1875. By 1891, it had 55 students from nearby *bastis*. The last fact is important, indicating as it does the catchment area of the girl students of these missionary schools. The upper-and middle-class families of neither the Hindu nor the Muslim communities sent their daughters to these schools. Their fears, as we have argued earlier, were that of proselytization and degradation of Indian values.

In such circumstances, the need was for a school for girls that would be truly Indian in character, preserve Indian traditions and remove all apprehensions of devaluing the Indian system. Accepting the challenge, some philanthropists of Delhi organized themselves to lay the foundation of Indraprastha School for girls in Delhi in 1904. This school, the root of Indraprastha College, was a product of the national struggle for women's education and has made a seminal contribution to women's education in Delhi.

The school, in fact, was founded at a crucial juncture of the anti-imperialist national struggle. It coincided with the *swadeshi* movement throughout the country. The spirit of *swadeshi*, engendered in Bengal, acquired an all-India character largely through the efforts of Bal Gangadhar Tilak. Mass meetings were held to proclaim and pledge *swadeshi* or the use of Indian goods and boycott of British commodities. Foreign cloth was burnt in public places and shops selling foreign goods were picketed. The Government tried to suppress the involvement of the schools and colleges in this movement by threatening to withdraw their grants-in-aid or government affiliation, deny the students the right to compete for scholarships, or debar them from government service. Such warnings, however, rarely perturbed the students. Yet, another significant aspect of the movement was the active participation of women. Conservative, urban middle-class, homebound women joined the procession and picketing. Women's involvement in the national movement heralded the empowerment of women.

Surrounded by a fiery national environment and at a time when education for women was not only considered unnecessary and undesirable but also socially ostracized, Indraprastha School stood firm in its determination to perform its own kind of *swadeshi* activity viz. consolidation of women's education in Delhi. The founders of Indraprastha School, being nationalists and social reformists themselves, must have been inspired by the pioneers of women's education and social reformers like Ishwar Chandra Vidyasagar, Ranade, Pandita Ramabai, Raja Rammohan Roy, and others. However, it was Annie Besant, an Irish lady, a theosophist and tireless supporter of women's education, who ultimately motivated and galvanized them to establish Indraprastha School.

ANNIE BESANT, WOMEN'S EDUCATION AND INDRAPRASTHA SCHOOL

Annie Besant arrived in India in 1893, committed to educating women. Fully aware of Indian fears regarding Christian proselytizing, she was cautious even as she advocated education for women. To assure the Indian public that she upheld the values of Indian tradition, Annie Besant stressed upon the revival of oriental faiths especially Hinduism.[12] In 1893–94 she toured the Indian theosophical lodges to prompt and exhort its members to start schools for girls all over India. To gain public support during her tours, she spoke on Indian philosophy, indicating her personal preference for Indian religions. Her lectures on the religions of India, on India's culture and philosophy, particularly the series entitled 'Wake Up India', attracted many orthodox Brahmins to theosophy. Impressed and inspired by her commitment to Indian knowledge, many people joined her movement.

The educational work of Annie Besant was started at Banaras. Whenever she talked of education, whether of Indian youth in general or of women in particular, she emphasized the importance of religious instruction. Thus National Schools were established all over India under the auspices of the Society for the Promotion of National Education with the objectives of imparting the Indian system of education and acquainting the students with their own religion and culture. It was along these lines that the Central Hindu College was established at Banaras in 1898. Subsequently, on the same pattern, the Central Hindu Girls' School was started at Banaras in 1904.

The linkage of education to religion and the use of the term 'Hindu' in the names of the two institutions founded at Banaras are debatable. Such attitudes, from the current worldview, would establish that the ideas of Annie Besant were reactionary, that her attempts were to strengthen conservatism, and that they were a hurdle to breaking the shackles of tradition. But, if we evaluate her role in the context of the nineteenth and the early twentieth centuries, the arguments would be a little different. It cannot be denied that Annie Besant was a keen promoter of education for all Indians and women in particular. But she was conscious of the Indian apprehensions and bias against Christian missionary institutions. Indian parents were willing to consider English education for their sons but they remained hesitant about their daughters. They feared that if educated, their daughters would lose their purity, social values, and religious ideas. To fulfil her mission of educating Indian women and to coax them out of their homes, Besant had to be discreet about the character and the curriculum of the institutions that she started or inspired. Her objective was clear. By encouraging such institutions, she could assure the upper-and middle-class families of India that if their daughters attended these institutions, their religious identity, social values, and Indian upbringing would not be endangered. Religion and education consequently became strongly intertwined. Each community had to be motivated separately to educate their women. To mobilize the support of the Hindu public, these institutions were started for the Hindus along religious lines. It should, however, be observed that the founders were quite clear from the beginning that they were not establishing religious institutions meant only for the Hindus and neither did they practice any prejudice against any caste or community. Despite this, in their earlier years, these institutions rarely had any Muslim girl students. This may have been because most Muslim families, bound by a rigid *purdah* tradition, still preferred to educate their daughters at home. However, as these institutions began to assert their Indian identity and Indian values, even the Muslims began to send their daughters here to study. Whether Hindu or Muslim, the families' hesitations were the same, and these institutions allayed those hesitations.

It took Annie Besant almost a decade to win the confidence of the Hindu public to educate their women. It took a little longer to convince the Muslims to send their daughters to school. To convince the Indians of the necessity and indispensability of education for women, she made appeals in writing and through speeches in 1903. Her speech to the Theosophical Society in 1903 and the pamphlet entitled 'The Education of Indian Girls' emphasized the need for sustained efforts for the education and upliftment of Indian women. Through this pamphlet, she sought a wide publicity for Indian women's education and appealed to 'let it serve as the basis of a national movement for women's education'. The national movement for girls' education, she argued, was already being followed in a few small girls' schools, managed by the lodges of the Theosophical Society. But the movement, she said, must become wider along national lines; 'it must accept the general Indian conception of a woman's place in the national life, not the dwarfed modern view but the ancient ideal.' She urged the people to see in women, 'the mother, the wife or in some cases the learned and pious ascetic, the *brahmavadini* of older days'. She further explained that the national movement for the education of girls must be one that fulfils the national requirements and 'India needs nobly trained wives, mothers, educated teachers, educated for learned professions.'[13]

To emphasize the relevance of education for women and make it attractive and interesting in a way that would not violate the traditional norms but would encourage women to step out of their homes to study, Annie Besant laid down what she called the 'essentials of education'. They included : (a) religious and moral education; (b) literary education; (c) scientific education; (d) 'artistic' education; and (e) physical education. The religious and moral education imparted would depend on the community concerned. Literary education included knowledge of vernacular languages and literature. Apart from literary education, the girls, according to their religion, could opt for the study of any one classical language, choosing from Sanskrit, Arabic or Persian. Annie Besant's curriculum also included Indian history, Indian geography, and stories of 'sweetest and strongest women' in Indian history so that the girls may feel inspired by these 'noble women'. Using the notion of the bonds of sisterhood, Annie Besant advocated the learning of English. Knowledge of English, she argued, was necessary to expose Indian women to the outside world and in particular to their non-Indian counterparts. To emphasize the need for this interaction, Annie Besant said that many 'sympathetic English women seek to know their Indian sisters' and this could be made possible only with the learning of English. Scientific education, for Besant, included sanitary law, nutrition, simple medicines, first aid, cookery, and hygiene of the house. Aware of the domestic commitments of Indian women, she saw such education as strengthening their capabilities in that direction. 'Artistic' education would explore the aesthetic talents of Indian women but within the traditional confines, in music—both instrumental and vocal, with the focus being on learning the *vina* and singing of *shlokas*—drawing, painting, and needlework. Physical education related to awareness about health, not only for women but the entire family; stress was laid on exercises pertaining to the upkeep of health.[14]

An analysis of the basics of education suggested by Annie Besant may portray her as tradition-bound, home-oriented, and committed to making educated mothers and wives. By the present yardstick, these educational ideas appear obsolete, anti-radical, and detrimental to the growth of modern education among women. But could we have expected Annie Besant to commend radical education when education for women was almost considered blasphemous and there was an outcry whenever any woman ventured into a school or a college? In such circumstances, caution and discretion were important and fully cognisant of that, Annie Besant was able to draw out many girls into the educational sphere. And though treading discreetly, Annie Besant was not closed to the idea of radicalizing women. In fact, she was a thorough feminist, stressing upon women's rights. She spoke of 'opening women to the outside world', to achieve which she advocated learning of English by women. More significantly, she cautiously reprimanded patriarchy by urging that women could not be seen as 'the rival and competitor of men in public employment'.[15]

Annie Besant's commitment to women's issues and women's education inspired the foundation of Indraprastha Hindu Kanya Shikshalaya (more popularly known as Indraprastha Hindu Girls School) in Delhi in 1904. It is pertinent to note the speech of Annie Besant that motivated the founders amidst the thundering applause of the theosophists in 1903:

...we may be sure that Indian greatness will not return until Indian womanhood obtains a larger, a freer and a fuller life, for largely in the hands of Indian women must lie the redemption of India. The wife inspires or retards the husband; the mother makes or mars the child. The power of women to uplift or debase man is practically unlimited and man and woman must walk forward hand-in-hand to the raising of India, else will she never be raised at all... out of our schools and colleges shall grow the India of the future... the battle for the education of girls is just beginning and may *Ishwara* bless those who are the vanguard and all beneficent powers enlighten their minds and make strong their hearts.[16]

Though delivered with caution, this speech demonstrated Besant's vivid vision for Indian women. The members of the Indraprastha lodge of the Theosophical Society took up Annie Besant's mandate. These theosophists formed a working committee, later to be the Board of Trustees, to carry further the agenda of educating women by laying the foundation of Indraprastha School. This committee was significant for its diversity, including men from different walks of life—Rai Piyare Lal, a judge by profession, who was nominated the President; Lala Balkrishan Das, a banker, assumed office as Honorary Secretary; Lala Jugal Kishore, a government official, took charge as Honorary Treasurer; Lala Sultan Singh, banker and honorary magistrate, and Lala Bishambar Nath, executive engineer, Public Works Department. Although employed in the imperial service of the British Government, these members were nationalists to the core. They were also deeply influenced by the prevailing belief to serve the interests of their community and mobilize the support of the Hindu public for the education of their women before they embarked on a wider, national movement for the education of women.

THE BEGINNINGS OF INDRAPRASTHA SCHOOL

Indraprastha Hindu Girls School was quite similar in its conception to Central Hindu Girls School founded in Banaras by Annie Besant in the same year. To win the confidence of the Hindus and galvanize their support but above all to demonstrate that this school followed patterns different from missionary schools, Indraprastha School, initially opened only to the Hindu girls above the age of five, ensured strict *purdah*. As early as 1906, Brahmins, Kshatriyas, Kayasthas, Jains, and Vaishyas sent their daughters to this school. From 1908 onwards, the numbers swelled with girls from Khatri, Rajput, Jat and Sikh families joining the school. Yet another development occurred in 1924 when Muslim families began to send their daughters here.

Indraprastha School was started in a *haveli* (mansion) donated by Rai Balkrishan Das. Originally built in 1857 by Rais Bhajan Lal, the *haveli* was situated in Chhipiwara, a *mohalla* (locality) of old Delhi that extended from Kashmere Gate to Delhi Gate. It was decided to use the *haveli* as the school premises until such time as the school could afford to build another building. The school, however, continues to be housed in the same *haveli* even today. It was in this *haveli* that the Delhi chapter of the Theosophical Society had opened its office and a library in 1883.

The early years of the school were fraught with problems. In the early twentieth century, when educational patterns were still being evolved and developed, it was difficult to get qualified trained women teachers. The school management was not averse to hiring male teachers. But the parents resisted and threatened to withdraw their daughters from the school if men teachers were employed. The management had no option but to abandon its plan of hiring male teachers and search even more earnestly for women teachers. Understanding the prejudices of the parents and the predicament of the management committee, Annie Besant called upon Leonara G'meiner, an Australian theosophist, to come to India and serve as the Principal of the school. G'meiner, a dedicated follower of Annie Besant, complied. She came to India along with her niece, O. James, in 1905 and was Principal of the school from that year onwards, and then of both the school and the college from 1924 to 1934. James, also a theosophist and a qualified kindergarten teacher, was made the head of the infant department.

Lack of funds for the school was a problem from the beginning. Struggling against financial odds, the founders decided to maintain the school by income derived from private subscriptions and donations and a grant from public funds. For instance, Lala Jugal Kishore, one of the founders, and a prime motivator in the running of the school and subsequently the college, had no hesitation in asking for donations at public or social functions—whether it was a marriage ceremony or a prize distribution day in the school. With the objective of consolidating funds, the founders initiated a plan of not only interacting with Hindu families but also other educational institutions in Delhi. In 1907, they appealed to the students of St. Stephen's Mission College to make a contribution to celebrate their success in the University examination. A significant donor from amongst the many students of St. Stephen's College who contributed was Shri Ram Kishore, who later played a major role not only in the life of Indraprastha College but also Delhi University. To further strengthen the financial base, a permanent endowment fund was floated. It began as a One-Rupee Fund in 1907 with a plea to the Hindus to make a contribution for the sake of the 'Hindu religion'. The founders, in their appeal, urged that while many Hindus made donations for the *dharamshalas*, there could 'surely be no better place of *dharma* than a school house... .'[17] The school struggled along with the help of private donations and funds until some hope dawned in 1913, when the Inspector of Schools recommended a Delhi Municipal Grant to the school whereby the Municipal Board promised to bear one-half of the expenditure of the school.

To attract the maximum number of girls, the school attempted to bond home life with school life. The students were taught in Hindi and religious and moral education to the Hindu girls was imparted according to the tenets of Sanatan Dharma. Apart from Hindi reading and writing and moral instruction, the emphasis was on needlework, drawing, music, cookery, hygiene, and physical education.

The curriculum followed the scheme of studies prescribed by the Punjab Education Department for Hindi schools with powers to the management to modify it. The Quarterly Reports of Indraprastha School indicate that the subjects introduced in 1904 were not merely to cater to the docile and domestic upbringing of the girls but with the specific purpose of strengthening and sharpening their physical and mental abilities. For instance, the objective of physical education was to improve the physique of the girls. Drawing, painting, and needlework, taught in classes II and III, were introduced to stimulate the faculty of observation and achieve greater steadiness and neatness. To expose the girls to the wider developments in the country and arouse their eagerness for knowledge, the school library subscribed to *Panchal Pandita*, a magazine that provided the girls information on the progress of women's education in India.

DEVELOPMENT AND CONSOLIDATION

By June 1910, almost within six years, there were not only a large number of Hindu families sending their daughters to Indraprastha School, there was also an unprecedented demand for the teaching of the English language. Conscious of the bias against the English language, the Board of Trustees were cautious in evolving a policy for the learning of English. No girl was allowed to join the English classes until she could satisfactorily read in the vernacular language. Secondly, English learning was introduced only from class III and since it was taught on request, the students who wished to learn it had to pay a special fee of Re 1 per month or such fees as the school authorities may fix from time to time, according to the expenses related to the teaching of English. With the dearth of women teachers equipped to teach the English language, the teaching of English in those days was quite expensive. Still the demand grew and the school was hard put to find women teachers for the purpose. However, one of the teachers on whom the school could depend was O. James who taught English in the Upper Primary Department by the direct method without books. Another credit that James brought to the school was the introduction of the Montessori system of teaching for the infant department. This idea was implemented for the first time in any school of Delhi.

It was not just English language teachers that the school had problem finding, women teachers who met the criteria for the various subjects were hard to come by. In 1906, apart from G'meiner, there were just two Brahmin lady teachers. The emphasis on the caste and gender of the teachers is noteworthy. This trend was peculiar to not only Indraprastha School but to all Hindu girls' schools in those days. Such rigidities created obstacles for the teaching of at least some subjects. For instance, at its foundation, Indraprastha School had committed itself to the teaching of the tenets of Sanatan Dharma but it could not do so in its earlier years as the parents resisted the school's proposal of engaging the services of a learned *pandit*. Similarly, hygiene and cookery classes could not be initiated for the lack of trained Hindu women teachers.

The problem of securing Hindu women teachers remained acute throughout the early years of the school. To resolve the situation, the school sent out public appeals for both trained and untrained teachers. For sometime in 1907, Leonara G'meiner was the sole staff member with the 'whole work thrown upon herself struggling with the tedium of language'.[18] Of the two Brahmin teachers, one had resigned owing to ill health and the other, much younger in age, had reportedly 'left for private reasons'.[19] The appeal for Hindu women teachers was sent out to not only the public of Delhi but also to some north Indian towns like Jalandhar, Amritsar, and Lahore, where the education for women had started much earlier as compared to Delhi. It was the Principal of Victoria Girls' School, Lahore, who provided Indraprastha School the services of two of her teachers—Bindu Bashini Devi, a Bengali Brahmin lady, who was a trained and middle-school-passed teacher; and Sant Devi, also a Brahmin but an untrained teacher. By

1908, the teaching faculty showed some expansion—there was one trained and three untrained teachers although the necessity of trained teachers was acutely felt in the lower classes.

Most trained teachers were Christians but the bias against them was strong. Fighting such prejudices, and particularly if they pertained to women's education, was not an easy task in those days. However, Indraprastha School displayed remarkable grit and determination in overcoming these reactions. Choosing pragmatism over irrationalities, the School appointed L. Burton, T. Mandal, and S. Mitra from Madras and Bombay Universities as teachers. By now the resistance against male teachers had also weakened. When, despite serious efforts, no *panditani* could be found to teach Sanskrit, the parents conceded that a *pandit* could be employed provided he was an elderly person. The obsession of the girls' parents with the caste and gender of the teachers was waning by 1924 as the school matured into an intermediate college. By then, there were two men teachers—Professor Rama Deva taught Hindi, Sanskrit, and philosophy and Pandit Nand Kishore taught music. A subsequent significant development was the employment of a Muslim male teacher, Rahman-ul-Nisa, to teach embroidery and needlework.

Another problem confronting the founders in the first decade of the school's existence was the irregular attendance of the students, or their leaving the school after a few months or after their primary education. Many girls stayed at home for a few months without any definite reasons and several promising pupils were married off early, putting an abrupt stop to their academic life. It was estimated that the average attendance was low owing to the early marriage of the girls. Some of them were married at the tender age of ten or eleven after attending school for a few months. In fact, invariably by class VI, the number of students dwindled on account of early marriage. By then, the girls were considered too old to attend school. The school authorities found it extremely difficult to convince the parents of the importance of education for their daughters even if it meant delaying their marriage. Nonetheless, the authorities kept up the pressure and constantly appealed to the parents to abandon rigid customs and become more alert towards their daughters' education. Shanti Devi, a former student of the school, recollects that when she was 14 or 15 years of age and in class VIII, her marriage was fixed. She was a good student who always stood first in class, and was expected to get a position in the Board examination. Lala Jugal Kishore requested her father (who incidentally was his friend) to postpone the marriage which coincided with the Board examination. The father expressed his apprehensions and suggested that he (Jugal Kishore) should speak to her prospective father-in-law. The latter, unconvinced of the values of women's education, dismissed the appeal. Though he expressed his happiness on getting an educated *bahu* (daughter-in-law), he said that he was not interested in her certificate. So, despite Lala Jugal Kishore's efforts, Shanti Devi had to leave school, abandon her education, and get married.[20] Shanti Devi's short encounter with school education testifies to the adamant approach of Hindu families towards the traditional pattern of early marriages and the education of their daughters. However, the efforts of people like Lala Jugal Kishore spelled hope for the education of women, married women in particular. He admitted his daughter-in-law to the school and ensured that she was educated.

As a tactic to persuade the parents, the management committee announced a scheme of scholarships. It also instituted prizes worth Rs 10 for punctuality and regularity The first student to be awarded the prize in this category was Ram Piyari, a student of class V in 1908. She was absent only once in 1906 and had never failed any class. As an additional incentive (especially when the parents may have hesitated to pay for their daughter's education), no admission or tuition fee was charged in the first ten years of the school's existence. Ironically, an admission fee of 8 annas was imposed in 1913 to control the increasing number of students. By 1913, the numbers had swelled to such an extent that the building was bursting at its seams. The fee was further enhanced to Re 1 in 1918 when the problem of accommodation and finances became even more acute.

Constraints of space and funds notwithstanding, the founders remained consistently vigilant to ensure that parents did not withdraw their daughters from the school. There were constant reminders that the school provided education to girls within the precincts of *purdah*. Demonstrating that their pledge was serious, the founders organized *ghoda garis* (horse carts) to fetch the girls from their homes to school and back, escorted by a *mahri* (maid). With the increasing number of students and also to cater to the girls coming from distant areas—right up to New Delhi—bus services with curtains were introduced in 1913.

Leonara G'meiner, along with Lala Jugal Kishore, kept up the effort of drawing as many girls as possible to the school and strengthening the argument against early marriages. To quote G'meiner, 'when will the people of India realize that youth is a period for physical, intellectual, moral and spiritual training and shall be free from the excitements and developments which belong to a mature period... .'[21] She endeavoured to bring consciousness towards education not only amongst men but also inspire women to understand the benefits of education. Such feelings became increasingly prevalent throughout the nation. It was realized that no amount of persuasion or legislation could bring a drastic change in social customs and traditions unless the women themselves were made aware of the need for reform and education. With this objective, Indraprastha Istri Sudhar Sabha was established in 1914. It was exclusively a women's association, comprising women from the families of the students, who, it was hoped, would help the school in many ways as only women can.

The efforts of Lala Jugal Kishore and Leonara G'meiner yielded positive results. By 1915, the objection to married girls attending school was weakening. Many girls were now regular in their attendance. Still, it was felt that only if the marriages of the girls were delayed could there be a desirable change in their school-going habits. Early marriages at the age of ten or eleven and the vast difference in age between husband and wife had virtually imposed widowhood on the young girls, who were denied a normal life. The Widow Remarriage Act passed in 1856 had barely yielded positive results. By 1890, there were only 500 widow remarriages. Rigid customs and parental objections had prevented even a reformer such as Ranade from marrying a widow. Such attitudes had compelled Rammohan Roy, Ishwar Chandra Vidyasagar, and D.K. Karve to labour even more to improve the status of widows. They argued that many widows who would not think of marrying again, would, if given the opportunity, avail the benefits of education. Karve argued, 'Why not then take up the work of providing educational facilities for the widows? After all, the object is to enable them to have a new and happy life.'[22] It is in this context that we must assess the changing attitude of Hindu families towards young widows in the mid-twentieth century. The stigma against widowhood continued but the thinking of the parents showed a positive change. They were now keen to educate their young widowed daughters and ensure their economic independence.

The changed attitude of the parents was one of the reasons for the opening of Matriculation classes or High School in Indraprastha School in 1916. By 1916, there was a notable increase in applications for admission by young widows, whose parents were anxious to qualify them for an independent living—an important transformation since 1904. Responding to the urge for higher education, the school prepared itself for the introduction of Matriculation classes. These classes were inspired by yet another significant development in Delhi—the opening of Lady Hardinge Medical College for Women in 1916. The establishment of this college generated an increasing demand from women for admissions in the school and its hostel. As in Victorian Edinburgh, a Matriculation degree was the minimum requirement for studying medicine in Delhi.

Struggling through financial stringency, the school geared itself to introduce Matriculation classes. It received a government grant for the purpose but financial scarcities remained. The school needed at least Rs 25,000 for starting these classes. To collect the sum, the Matriculation Classes Endowment Fund was created, to which many philanthropists from Delhi and Lahore contributed.[23] The most valuable contributions—financial and emotional—were made by two prominent women—renowned poet and patriot Sarojini Naidu and Kamla Nehru, wife of Pandit Jawaharlal Nehru. The latter, incidentally was a pupil of the school in its early days.

The fact that Matriculation classes were successful and that they contributed to making women confident and forthcoming is evident from an article published in a magazine in 1929. It says that in 1918 for the first time a married student passed her matriculation from the school. After this, the girl graduated from Banaras Hindu University and carried out admirable work in the field of women's education in Bihar.[24]

By 1916, the school's popularity had spread beyond Delhi. During this year, a large number of girls from states like Bengal, Madras, and Punjab joined the school. Indeed a sign of success for women's education, though it created an extraordinary situation for the school—several of these students did not know Hindi. There was thus a proposal for starting a Anglo-vernacular high school. Once the decision was taken, there was no delay in its implementation. It was applied in the same year, that is, 1916. The students after class V were given the option of continuing their studies either in the vernacular language in the middle school or were drafted into the English department, where all subjects were taught in English, and Hindi was continued as a special subject. By 1918, English was made the medium of instruction in High School. Within five years, that is, by 1923, the demand for the teaching of English had grown more intense. Consequently, it began to be taught as one of the regular subjects and formed a part of the curriculum from class IV onwards. Although every student of the school was now expected to learn English, the school refrained from arbitrary impositions for fear of alienating parents. Therefore, if any parent objected to the learning of English by their daughter, they were permitted to withdraw them from the subject.

Such developments encouraged the school management to dream of raising the school into an all-India Hindu Girls' college. College it did grow into in 1924, with the opening of Intermediate classes, and not merely for Hindi girls. It was open to all castes and communities, with no economic barriers. From its beginning, the college took some radical stands. For instance, Leonara G'meiner made gradual but successful attempts at removing the tradition of *purdah*. Her plea against early marriages also yielded positive results. By the 1930s, out of over 600 girls (from 5 years to 24 years of age) in the Indraprastha institutions—both school and college—there were only two or three girls who were married.

LEONARA G'MEINER, HOME RULE LEAGUE, AND THE SCHOOL

The evolutionary years of the school coincided with the growing national fervour for independence as well as the constant attempts of the British Government to consolidate its power and legitimacy. The year 1911 marked a significant landmark in Indian politics and in the life of Delhi in particular. The Government, not able to withstand violent national agitation, was forced to withdraw the partition of Bengal in 1911. More significantly for Delhi, in the same year, the capital was shifted from Calcutta to Delhi. Delhi also became the cynosure with the elaborate coronation ceremony of George V on 22 June, 1911.

The coronation celebrations may have been impressive but they were definitely transitory. By 1914, the nation had become even more restless and resistant towards government policies. It was realized that unless there was a mass movement or unless popular pressure was applied on the Government, it would not make any concessions. The direction to the national movement during these years was provided by the two Home Rule Leagues started in 1915-16, one under the leadership of Lokmanya Tilak and the other by Annie Besant and S. Subramanya Iyer. The two Home Rule Leagues carried out an intense propaganda against the British Government and demanded the grant of Home Rule or self-government to India definitely after the war.

When the Home Rule Movement started, Delhi was virtually politically dead. There was no political organization with any dynamic programme for arousing the dormant consciousness of the people. It was Leonara G'meiner, the Principal of Indraprastha School, who took the lead in bringing this movement to Delhi. Anxious to implement the order of her spiritual and political *guru* Annie Besant, G'meiner along with other supporters started the branch of the Home Rule League in Delhi. It was formally inaugurated on 20 February, 1917 and G'meiner was appointed its Honorary Secretary.[25] She and her friend, Miss Priest, a voluntary worker in the school, spent hours in the office of the League everyday after finishing the work of the school. Soon the office hummed with activity, attracting enthusiasts eager to join the movement. The audience at the meetings of the League reportedly 'sometimes swelled to twenty thousand'.[26] It was with remarkable courage and diligence that G'meiner mobilized the support of both the intellectuals and the masses of Delhi. In her later years, she often recalled that heady period with fondness as, 'Oh, those wonderful days!'[27]

The popularity of the Home Rule Movement in Delhi and the success of Leonara G'meiner obviously found no favour with the local authorities of Delhi. The Government expressed its displeasure at G'meiner's involvement in the Home Rule League activities in Delhi, by targetting the school. The school, 'a wholly innocuous and an admittedly admirable institution' was threatened with a variety of victimization.[28] Another tactic adopted by the Delhi executive was organizing a 'crude campaign' of the Criminal Intelligence Department (CID) against the local Home Rule League. A description of the role adopted by the CID would help in understanding how the activities of the local Home Rule League were monitored. A friendly, anonymous CID official visited the League office everyday, sat till the closing hours of the office, helped Miss G'meiner 'to tidy up things, shut the doors etc. and then departed'.[29] CID officials also flooded the reading room of the Home Rule League. They not only occupied a 'disproportionate share of the available space' but also took an intense personal interest in the other 'non-official' visitors of the reading room by making intimate queries about their family history and other antecedents. To pry deeper into their lives, the CID officials would even sometimes accompany them to their homes. Such unpleasant encounters with the CID officials often intimidated the readers, compelling them to stop their visits to the reading room.[30]

Apart from using the CID to control and curb the activities of the Home Rule League in Delhi, the Chief Commissioner of Delhi sent constant warnings to the office-bearers of the League. These warnings were disguised as advice 'to desist from activities subversive to the tranquility of the Province'. Such advice and warnings, of course, fell on deaf ears. The Government then went ahead with banning public meetings of the League. Speakers were put under 'muzzling orders' (this was a favourite official expression in those days). The Home Rule Movement reached its climax in the trial of two speakers, Asaf Ali and Neki Ram Sharma, during which Leonara G'meiner appeared as an important witness. The Government was fuming at the active participation of G'meiner, yet she was not arrested—not because of any philanthropy on the Government's part but because the existing government policy did not permit the imprisonment of women. However, G'meiner and Indraprastha School were not to go unpunished.[31]

Hailey, the Chief Commissioner of Delhi, wasted no time in warning Lala Jugal Kishore, the Honorary Secretary of Indraprastha School, that Leonara G'meiner should either withdraw from the Home Rule League or resign as the Principal of the school.[32] As a coercive tactic, the Chief Commissioner organized a meeting with the Honorary Secretary along with G'meiner and Priest. G'meiner, keen to preserve the interests of the school and yet adamant over the issue of Home Rule League, reiterated to the Chief Commissioner her personal loyalty to Annie Besant and the League. She explained that no other member of the school's committee nor any other person connected with the school except Priest and herself were members of the Home Rule Movement. The Home Rule League had a separate identity from the school and in her opinion it was a 'perfectly legitimate movement'. However, these explanations failed to convince the Chief Commissioner. He dismissed them as mere arguments and stipulated that irrespective of the rules and regulations, people engaged in education should not participate in politics. He insisted that the Home Rule Movement in the case of persons connected with schools was distinctly 'wrong'. 'In fact,' he said, 'I consider the whole thing wrong.' Undeterred, G'meiner queried the Chief Commissioner on whether the Home Rule Movement was wrong. To that he said, 'it does not matter whether it is right or wrong, that is not the question; it is the opinion I have. You may think me to be very stupid, but that is how it stands.'[33]

Having made that arbitrary statement but also realizing its futility in impressing the school authorities to take any action against G'meiner, the Chief Commissioner threatened to withdraw his 'sympathy' from the school. Disdainful of his attitude, Indraprastha School Committee inquired whether the withdrawal of 'sympathy' would affect the municipal grants-in-aid to the school. The unmoved Chief Commissioner responded indifferently: 'You can interpret that as you like.' He further added 'it was not a question of opinion but of administration' and that in this particular case he happened 'to hold the handle of the knife.'[34] And, he undoubtedly did, which is apparent from his letter to the Deputy Commissioner of Delhi, instructing him to stop grants from the municipal funds to Indraprastha School 'until receipt of a further communication from us.'[35] Apart from the grants-in-aid, the payment of scholarship money was also withheld, causing direct and uncalled-for injustice to over 350 students. To prove that the consequences could be worse if the government orders were not followed, Indraprastha students, unlike the girls of other Delhi schools, were not allotted an evening in a week to visit the gardens of the Red Fort. The Inspector of Schools had begun to organize such visits for girls from Delhi schools.[36]

The Honorary Secretary of Indraprastha School protested against these developments. He argued that even if the Government wished to punish the school by withdrawing the grant, there were no reasons for the education department to derecognize the school. Derecognition, he insisted, was particularly unfair since the school had maintained its efficiency under the prescribed rules. He reiterated that the issue of giving grants-in-aid was separate from recognition. Recognition may be necessary before any grants-in-aid were sanctioned but certainly not the other way round.[37]

Indraprastha School's harassment because of the involvement of its Principal in the Home Rule Movement cannot be dismissed as an isolated, specific example. Its impact was felt not merely on the society of Delhi but nationwide. National newspapers such as *The Tribune*, *Bombay Chronicle*, and *New India*, particularly of the months of May and June 1917, carried exhaustive items on Indraprastha School. The issues pertaining to the school were raised at the meeting of the legislative council of the Governor-General of India held on 24 September, 1917. In response to all queries—whether regarding the withdrawal of grants-in-aid or the scholarship money or the weekly evening jaunts to the Red Fort gardens, or the assurances of Leonara G'meiner about her role in the Home Rule Movement and separate identities of the League and the school—the representative of the Chief Commissioner, Sir William Vincent, justified the Government's moves. He defended the withdrawal of the grants-in-aid and the scholarship money by arguing that it was contrary to public policy that teachers of schools enjoying grants-in-aid from public money should take a prominent part in political agitation. Therefore, unless G'meiner withdrew from active participation in the work of the League, the withdrawal of the grant would continue. Since the grants-in-aid were withdrawn, the school became 'unrecognized' according to the education code. Consequently, the payment of scholarship fund was also stopped. For the ban on the weekly Red Fort outings, he blamed the Inspector of Schools. He argued that neither was this matter discussed with the local administration nor did the local government pass any orders on this issue. Sir Vincent made yet another insinuation, this time regarding the Honorary Secretary of the school. He stated that the Honorary Secretary had informally explained to the Chief Commissioner that the work of the League was separate from that of the school. More significantly, Sir Vincent claimed that even the Honorary Secretary did not approve of the Principal's active involvement with the Home Rule League.[38] These allegations were aimed at creating a rift between the Honorary Secretary and G'meiner. But Vincent failed in his strategy since the school committee neither compelled G'meiner to resign from the Home Rule League nor from the school. Instead, they appealed to the Chief Inspector of Schools, Delhi, to provide Indraprastha School affiliation with the Punjab University. The Inspector, however, declined to do so, since the Government had derecognized the school.[39]

The school authorities preferred to forego the entire grant rather than dismiss Leonara G'meiner. To consolidate the school finances in the absence of any assistance from the Government, the management committee organized itself to collect funds from not only the citizens of Delhi but also from beyond Delhi by issuing appeals through newspapers and private contacts. Emboldened rather than weakened by the lack of government support, the school continued to be run privately by the Indraprastha Registered Society. To meet the deficits, the committee borrowed money from Allahabad Bank, Delhi, and the school's Permanent Endowment Fund, which appeared increasingly insufficient by 1918. An addition of a lakh of rupees to the Permanent Endowment Fund seemed to be the only means of survival. Lala Jugal Kishore, spearheaded the drive for the collection of funds. One of his suggestions was that the Society for the Advancement of Indraprastha Hindu Girls' High School, Delhi should put forward a scheme for the collection of Rs 5000. He suggested that Re 1 each could be collected from 5000 persons, especially women, on the occasion of different festivals. His proposal was motivated by the fact that if women sympathized with their own cause, the change and the improvement in the status of women and their education would be faster. A poignant feature during this crisis was that despite the intensity of financial bankruptcy none of the individual donors withdrew their subscription from the school's endowment fund, neither did any student leave the school. This shows the immense faith and trust that Indraprastha School had built amongst the citizens of Delhi.

Leonara G'meiner left no stone unturned to bring the issue of Indraprastha School to the mainstream of Indian politics. She used the media to expose the Government's arbitrary stand. In her letter to the editor of *Bombay Chronicle* she sought to remind 'the readers of other provinces that the bureaucracy in Delhi has held a firmer sway here than in other parts of India, so that the splendid action of the school committee shines out in greater radiance on account of the murky atmosphere of oppression in which it made its fearless decision.'[40]

The newspaper articles of 1917 establish that the issue of Indraprastha School was far from being a localized affair. *Bombay Chronicle,* in one of its items entitled 'Imperial Delhi', not only discussed the consequences arising out of G'meiner's involvement in the Home Rule League but was also openly critical of the Chief Commissioner's behaviour towards the school. The general feeling of anger and hostility against the Delhi Government is reflected in the article: 'That touch of Socratic humility (in Mr Hailey) could hardly have been accidental ... while it argues unsuspected grace in Mr.

Hailey ... The fact is that he is suffering from the consequences of prolonged indulgence in unchecked exercise of authority which has robbed him of all sense of proportion. The obsession of the first person singular is no uncommon phenomenon in respect of autocrats unable to sustain the weight of their powers and responsibility. Mr. Hailey ... has an imitative penchant for the grandiloquent...'[41] The reporter emphasized that the peculiar autocracy of the Chief Commissioner was not confined only to Indraprastha School. The fact that he suffered from general obsession of power and tyrannical pangs is evident from the excerpts of his interview with Maulana Muhammad Ali of *The Comrade*, in which he talked of the 'sword of the British Raj', of which the reporter said 'presumably Mr. Hailey fancied himself the custodian.'[42]

The case of Indraprastha School stirred many nationalists. For instance, Dr Tej Bahadur Sapru's concerns and queries on the role of Delhi Government vis-á-vis Indraprastha School were reported in *The Tribune* of 24 September, 1917. Dr Sapru wondered whether the Chief Commissioner of Delhi acted in pursuance of any general policy of the Government of India or on his own responsibility. The Government's response was prompt. In an attempt to acquit itself, the Government sought to make it clear that the Chief Commissioner of Delhi had not acted according to any general or particular instructions of the Government of India but on his own accord.[43] It is apparent from the statement of the government counsel that it did not matter if provincial governments were arbitrary; what was important was to bail out the Government of India and present it as the true upholder of Indian law and tradition and the sole legitimate power-wielding authority.

The Government's coercive tactics against the school did not succeed in compelling the management to compromise its stand towards the national movement. This is reflected in Lala Jugal Kishore's response to Gandhi's call for *swadeshi* and boycott of foreign cloth. As a government official in the Delhi Tramway and Electric Supply Traction Company, Lala Jugal Kishore was obliged to be loyal to the British Government. But, contrary to government expectations, Lala Jugal Kishore not only supported the participation of Leonara G'meiner in the Home Rule League but also boldly stood by Indraprastha School in those difficult times. He further infuriated the Government by wearing *swadeshi* garments to office. The Government warned him and insisted that he should abide by the government office norms, that is, dress in the prescribed way, or else he would be dismissed. Such threats proved meaningless to Lala Jugal Kishore. He offered to resign his government job rather than curb his nationalistic inclinations or abandon his efforts for women's education.[44] His son Lala Jagdish Prasad was no different. He also became a member and the Honorary Secretary of the managing committee of Indraprastha School and College. As a student, Jagdish Prasad had participated in the boycott of foreign cloth and promotion of *swadeshi*. Responding to Gandhi's call for *swadeshi*, he opened the first *swadeshi* cloth store in Chandni Chowk in Delhi, in which he suffered heavy financial losses. The demand for *swadeshi* cloth was probably still limited in 1919. Despite these losses, Lala Jagdish Prasad continued to promote the cause of *swadeshi*. He also sought to spread the nationalistic spirit amongst others by writing regular articles for the magazine *Harijan*[45] sponsored by Gandhi. Meanwhile, Indraprastha School moved steadily onwards, fighting numerous odds in its pioneering efforts for women's education.

NOTES AND REFERENCES

1. Uma Chakravarty, *Rewriting History: The Life and Times of Pandita Ramabai*, Kali for Women in association with The Book Review Literary Trust, New Delhi, 1998, p. ix.

2. Shaista Suhrawardy Ikramullah, *From Purdah to Parliament*, p. 27.

3. Gauri Srivastava, 'The Contribution of Male Intelligentsia to Women's Education in Bombay Presidency during the Colonial Period', in Sabyasachi Bhattacharya (ed.), *The Contested Terrain*, p. 275.

4. Partha Chatterjee, 'The Nation and Its Women', in Ranajit Guha (ed.), *A Subaltern Studies Reader, 1986–1995*, Oxford University Press, New Delhi, 1998, p. 253.

5. Sambuddha Chakrabarty, *Antare Andare*, p. 59.

6. Partha Chatterjee, 'The Nation and Its Women', p. 249.

7. Ibid., pp. 252–5

8. Dhananjay Keer, *Jotirao Phooley: Father of the Indian Social Revolution*, Popular Prakashan, Bombay, 1964, pp. 23 ff.

9. Uma Chakravarty, *Rewriting History*, p. 73.

10. Gauri Srivastava, 'The Contribution of Male Intelligentsia to Women's Education', pp. 283–6

11. Partha Chatterjee, 'The Nation and Its Women', pp. 253–4.

12. See Nita Kumar, 'Why does Nationalist Education Fail? The Case of Banaras from the 1880s to the 1930s', in Sabyasachi Bhattacharya (ed.), *The Contested Terrain*, p. 90.

13. 'The Education of Indian Girls', Speech of Annie Besant in 1903 to the Theosophical Society of India.

14. Ibid.

15. Ibid.

16. Ibid.

17. Lady Superintendent's Report in The Fifth Half Yearly Report of Indraprastha Hindu Kanya Shikshalaya, 30 June, 1908.

18. Lady Superintendent's Report in The Half Yearly Report of Indraprastha Hindu Kanya Shikshalaya, 30 June, 1907.

19. Ibid.

20. Shanti Devi, 'Istri Shiksha Ko Apne Paer Per Khara Kiya', in Founder's Birth Centenary Souvenir, Indraprastha Girls Higher Secondary School, 1978.

21. Lady Superintendent's Report in The Half Yearly Report of Indraprastha Hindu Kanya Shikshalaya, 30 June, 1907.

22. Gauri Srivastava, 'The Contribution of Male Intelligentsia to Women's Education', p. 279.

23. Matriculation Classes Endowment Fund, Indraprastha School, April 1916.

24. 'Indraprastha Girls School and College', *Chand*, Allahabad, September 1929.

25. Letter to the Editor entitled 'Delhi Chief Commissioner and the Girls School' by Leonara G'meiner in response to widely published letters 'CID and Politics' and 'Official Campaign against Home Rule in Delhi', *Bombay Chronicle*, 7 June, 1917.

26. 'Miss G'meiner: A Life Dedicated to Service', *The Hindustan Times*, 23 April, 1934.

27. Ibid.

28. 'Imperial Delhi', *Bombay Chronicle*, 12 June, 1917.

29. 'Miss G'meiner: A Life Dedicated to Service'.

30. 'Imperial Delhi'.

31. 'Miss G'meiner: A Life Dedicated to Service'.

32. Letter to the Editor entitled 'Delhi Chief Commissioner and the Girls School'.

33. Ibid. Also, 'Imperial Delhi'.

34. Letter to the Editor entitled 'Delhi Chief Commissioner and the Girls School'.

35. From the Chief Commissioner, Delhi to Deputy Commissioner, Delhi, Copy of a letter No. 3267, Education, 26 April, 1917.

36. Letter to the Editor entitled 'Delhi Chief Commissioner and the Girls School'.

37. Honorary Assistant Secretary, Indraprastha Hindu Girls High School to Mrs. V. Gilbertson, Assistant Superintendent of Female Education, Delhi Province, Education, 19 May, 1917.

38. Questions to be asked by the Hon'ble Kamini Kumar Chanda at the meeting of the Legislative Council of the Governor General of India, held on 24 September, 1917 and the Reply by the Hon'ble Sir William Vincent, Proceedings Legislative Council, 1917.

39. Letter to the Editor entitled 'Delhi Chief Commissioner and the Girls School'.

40. Ibid.

41. 'Imperial Delhi'.

42. Ibid.

43. 'Indraprastha Girls School', *The Tribune*, 28 September, 1917.

44. Sarla Sharma, 'Birth of Indraprastha', in Founder's Birth Centenary Souvenir, Indraprastha Girls Higher Secondary School, 1978.

45. 'Unflinching Dedication to Indraprastha: A Name To Be Remembered In The Field Of Education' (unpublished), from the Archives of Indraprastha Girls Higher Secondary School.

2

Matrimony After Matriculation? Breaking the Pattern, 1924–32

The path to higher education for women, at least till the first quarter of the twentieth century, had remained thorny. However, missionaries and Bengali social reformers such as Vidyasagar had persisted in their efforts to impart some modicum of literacy to women. Their sustained efforts had created a situation wherein by the last decades of the nineteenth century there were a few Bengali women, albeit from enlightened Brahmo families, who were ready to enter a university. Securing a degree still remained a difficulty because at first women were not allowed to sit for examinations at the University. In 1878, the Senate allowed women to sit for examinations separately and under the supervision of women. Yet nine years later the vice chancellor could count only 23 women candidates for various courses. This signifies that societal opposition to higher education for women was keeping women away from college.

Towards Higher Education for Women

Domesticity was still regarded as the goal of women's lives. Aparna Basu recounts the disapproval expressed by Parvatibai Athavale towards the idea of women educating themselves for the sake of employment. Yet the widowed Parvatibai, at the age of 48, travelled to USA to study the English language.[1] It appears that in the initial stages, marital status, to a certain extent, determined the direction of the slow march of the Indian women towards higher education. A slight advance towards liberal ideas was made in so far as elementary education for women was concerned since young Indian men preferred literate wives. Elementary education for women was seen as a necessity for the ideal of 'companionate marriage'. The 'frightening lack of female education' was expressed humorously in 1929 in a magazine published from Allahabad: 'If the husband is a BA, LLB passed expert lawyer, the wife is a BA in grinding spices and LLB of cowpat.'[2] The article points out the dangers of such a mismatched marriage: the uneducated wife will lose her husband either to a second wife or to a concubine. The article referred to Delhi's Indraprastha College as an institution that was helping society to confront this problem by providing education for women.[3]

Resistance to higher education for women was on the decline by the second decade of the twentieth century. Heralding the trend, Madras Medical College and Bombay Medical College admitted women in 1878 and 1883 respectively, for the first time. Indian women studied medicine either in India (Madras and Bombay) or by going abroad. By 1902, 242 women were attending medical schools and many were trained as teachers, nurses, and midwives. 'Education,' comments Kumari Jayawardene, 'enabled some women to break into avenues of employment that had previously been denied to them'.[4] The Indian orthodox opinion, however, could not tolerate women and men medical students studying together. Yet the need for lady doctors was becoming increasingly pressing for the health and well-being of the country's female population. In the early years of the twentieth century, the vicereine Lady Hardinge took personal interest in the cause of medical training for Indian women. Under her leadership a fund collection initiative was begun. When the medical college for women was established in Delhi in 1916, it was named after the vicereine who had been instrumental in its being born. In the beginning there were 14 students in Lady Hardinge Medical College for Women and teachers were brought from England by the All India Medical Services. At first, like other colleges in Delhi such as St. Stephen's and Hindu, this college too was affiliated to Punjab University. By 1930, there were 113 students, 89 of them Indian.

Teaching, however, was the most favoured career for women. This was a heartening change, since in the beginning, the cause of female education in north India had suffered from the lack of trained or even educated women teachers. As early as 1882, G.W. Leitner of the University of Punjab had declared that female teachers and inspectors were necessary to attract girls from middle and upper classes to schools.[5] Padmini Swaminathan, in an article on women's education in colonial Tamil Nadu between 1900 to 1930, mentions a report that stressed the need to appoint women on the staff, particularly beyond Class III. The report found that of the girls who joined schools staffed by men teachers, very few continued to read beyond Class III.[6] Therefore to introduce compulsory education for girls between the ages of five and ten, it was essential to establish schools for girls with women teachers. Since such were the compulsions in the Madras Presidency, which, along with Bengal and Bombay, was progressive where western education is concerned, it is not surprising that in conservative north India the attitude regarding women teachers would be rigid. At the turn of the century the Bengali Boys School in Delhi permitted girls to join the school. But after Class III, by a special arrangement, the girls shifted to Indraprastha School.

Christian mission schools, operating in Delhi since before the mutiny, could have solved the problem regarding women teachers. That this did not transpire is explained by Maskiell, writing about colonial Punjab, (see the Introduction) and Swaminathan, writing about colonial Madras. Swaminathan quotes from a letter written by the Director of Public Education in 1913: 'We must look to the class of widows for our supply of caste women teachers...since the alternative, the employment of Indian Christian women is repugnant to popular feelings.'[7] However, Rama Mehta, who has made a study of the western educated Hindu woman, writes that with regard to the attitude towards mission schools there was some change by the 1920s and 1930s. A few thoroughly westernized fathers preferred to send their daughters to mission schools.[8]

That there had occurred a change in Indian society regarding higher education for women is reflected in a table provided by Swaminathan showing sex-wise disparity in the various grades of education. Moving from 1911–12 to 1926–27, we find the ratio of male to female students in the arts colleges of Madras changing from 106:1 to 24:1.[9] The gap had reduced considerably. The same finding is reflected in a table giving a religion-wise break-up of Lahore's Kinnaird College for Women by Michelle Maskiell, which begins with the same years as in Swaminathan's table. In 1913-14 there were only 65 Hindu students in Kinnaird College, whereas by 1929–47 there were 672 students. That is, from comprising 35% of the total student population they were now 51%.[10] According to Aparna Basu, the beginning of the 1920s showed an encouraging growth in women's college education in Bombay. In 1921–22, there were 258 girls in colleges, of whom 179 were in arts and 79 in professional colleges.[11] The 1920s, which are the significant closing years in both tables referred to above, and also quoted by Basu as well, is the very period in which Intermediate classes were inaugurated (in 1924) at Indraprastha School in Delhi. Thus Indraprastha College came into being just when all over the country there was a stir in the world of higher education for women. At the time the first women's college in Delhi for the study of liberal arts was begun, there were four other colleges existing in Delhi—the old Anglo-Arabic College at Ajmeri Gate (the present Zakir Hussain College), St. Stephen's, Hindu, and Ramjas. All these predated the establishment of Delhi University, which was established in 1922. Until then, these colleges remained affiliated to Punjab University.

A 'COSMOPOLITAN' COLLEGE

The growth of Indraprastha College was closely related to the changing character of the city of Delhi. By the 1920s Delhi was well established as the new capital of India. Government officers from all over India were arriving in Delhi. The number of officials working in western firms also increased. Generally, people who had come into contact with either government service or western commercial houses were not averse to the idea of a modern education for the women in their families. Daughters of the officials transferred to Delhi from other cities needed to complete their education. Indraprastha was their only alternative if they did not wish to join mission schools or colleges.

The Admissions and Withdrawals Register of 1925–47 of Indraprastha College, an interesting document, yields fascinating insights into the sociological and cultural developments taking place in the Indian society in this early modern phase of the colonial period. That certain old habits still persisted is evident from the scrupulous attention paid to the recording not only of religious beliefs but also castes of the students admitted. One might hazard an opinion that perhaps due to the Arya Samaj movement Hindus had become self-conscious about how they defined themselves. It might also be possible that due to the same factor there was a certain degree of confusion as to their origins. Apart from the recital of the usual caste names such as Brahmin, Kayastha, Khatri, Vaishya, Brahmos, we have interesting variations such as Aryan Vaishyas, Brahmo-Hindu, or just simply Vedic or Arora, the last of which is not the name of a caste. The person who wrote just Arora was perhaps protesting against the rigid hold of the caste system in India. In 1938–39 we find an entry by one Bal Kishan Das of Delhi, who boldly declares himself a non-Hindu, but cautiously notes down 'of Brahmin origin'. In that same period we discover among the Muslim families admitting their daughters into college a similar desire to declare in their antecedents their family pride or aspirations. In 1938–39 one parent declared himself 'Mughal' in the caste column.

The first Muslim student of the college Tehzib Sarbuland Jang, daughter of Nawab Sarbuland Jang of Delhi, joined in 1930. So far as occupations were concerned, the Nawab fitted into the prevailing profile of parents willing to give their daughters an opportunity for college education. These were overwhelmingly professionals such as doctors, barristers, academics, and government officials. Nawab Sarbuland Jang was an advocate. Between 1924 to 1930 there were nine doctors, four law professionals, five teachers, and one engineer who admitted their daughters to Indraprastha College. High-ranking as well as ordinary levels of government functionaries were also eager to avail of the opportunity to educate their daughters. The college had admitted the daughter of a member of the Public Service Commission and the daughter of the Accountant General, GPO. There were also stationmasters and clerks who sent their daughters to college. Men who belonged to the business class were more reticent in allowing women of their families contact with western education. In the first batch of seven students appearing in the college examination in 1925, only one was the daughter of businessman, a contractor. In 1926 another businessman had sent his daughter to college. In 1928–30, two more fathers listed as merchants sent their daughters to college.

In the column which listed the places from where the students hailed, we find the names of many small towns of north India, from the United Provinces and Punjab—Meerut, Khurja, Sonepat, Rohtak, Patiala, Jhansi, Kherwara, Rewari, Lucknow, Jaipur, Gurgaon, Muzaffarnagar. These towns had sent students to Indraprastha College between 1924 to 1930. Government officials transferred to Delhi from Calcutta and Berhampore in Bengal also sent their daughters to this newly established liberal arts college. An interesting place listed in the register is Simla-Delhi. This refers to the curious custom of the colonial government of shifting its capital to Simla during the summer months. Quite a few Delhi schools also shifted their establishments to Simla along with the Government for half of every year. The wide catchment area of Indraprastha College shows that the college fulfilled the needs of Indian society at a moment when it was undergoing social change, when the stirrings of social mobility were felt in all communities. Liberal Brahmo families such as the Majumdar family to which Sucheta Kripalani[12] belonged, sent their girls in the very first year of the college. But what is notable is the fact that after 1930, more and more Muslim students joined the college. Five new Muslim students were admitted by 1938–39. There were also a few Christian students, but these were perhaps girls who would not attend the boys' college at St. Stephen's.

The date of birth of the first seven students admitted in 1924 ranged from 1902 to 1908. Some of them were 22 years old when they entered the intermediate class. For them the establishment of a girls' college must have been a boon. The Admissions and Withdrawals Register also records a high rate of withdrawals. There could be two reasons for that. Some may have left to get married. Some others may have been daughters of government officials who were compelled to leave when their fathers were transferred due to the demands of government service.

The changes in the composition and thinking of the inhabitants of Delhi created the context and provided encouragement for the transformation of Indraprastha School into an intermediate college, and in 1925 it was recognized as an intermediate college. To invite applications from the students, the trustees advertised in the three national newspapers. That apart from *The Leader* and *The Hindustan Times*, *The Pioneer* of Lucknow was also included bears out the claim made in the advertisement: 'Being the only college for women in this province, it is expected to provide higher education for women in this part of the country.' The notice carefully stated: 'Though strictly a Hindu institution in its ideals and management, its doors are open to non-Hindu girls as well.' The advertisement clearly reveals the sensitivity of the trustees to the social and political climate in the capital. The analysis of the entries in the Admissions and Withdrawals Register of the college for the years 1924 to 1947 indicates the objectives of the founders. That the hopes of the founders were fulfilled is evident from the Principal's report of 1930 which mentions that, among 29 girls in the intermediate class, there was one Muslim and three Christian girls. Sarla Sharma, an old student of the college and granddaughter of one of the founders Lala Jugal Kishore, remembers that in the mid-1930s, a number of her Muslim classmates were active in national politics. The Muslim students in the college, with their rich cultural heritage, gave a unique flavour to the life in Indraprastha College. Muslim women unhesitatingly sought admission in this college since it promised to respect their privacy and scrupulously maintain the tradition of *purdah*. One of the students of the college in the years 1941–45 was Qurratullain Haider, the celebrated Urdu novelist and Sahitya Akademi awardee.

Indraprastha College continued to grow as a cosmopolitan institution, attracting women from all sections of the society, irrespective of their religion, caste, or economic status. From the beginning, scarcity of resources dogged its footsteps but it battled on valiantly. At times the founders had to take personal loans to run the college. From time to time there were dire financial crises, as in 1931, which stressed the ingenuity of the managing committee greatly. Yet its reaction in 1929, the silver jubilee year of the school, to the Government's order to levy fees from students was of dismay. The founders feared that deserving students might discontinue studies, thereby jeopardizing the rationality of the institution's founding. On the other hand, the colonial Government wanted to encourage self-sufficiency in education in India. The thinking was that education had not progressed in the country as the people had baulked at it being imposed on them. Communities were to be encouraged to support educational institutions in their midst. After the Government legislation to impose fees was passed, the Indraprastha College authorities had to decide what to charge from students. The college fee was fixed at Rs 5. To ensure that fee was not a disincentive for the girls, the management instituted a number of scholarships. The list of scholarships awarded in the college reflects the custom in Indian society at that time of identifying individuals by their castes. The categorization in the list reveals the upper-class orientation of the student body. At the beginning of the century this was the class which denied its women the benefits of education. The mission schools of the nineteenth century, valiant efforts as they were, could only draw upon the children who lived in poor localities, who because of their poverty could make little use of their education. Indraprastha School and College was successful in drawing out, apart from others, the strictly guarded daughters of upper-middle-class Indian families.

From the beginning, the college showed good examination results. Two of its students of the second batch of the intermediate class performed brilliantly, securing first divisions. Rajdulari of the first batch received the Makhanlal Gold Medal from the Vice Chancellor. She was the first woman recipient of the award. Later she became the Vice Principal of the college. Impressed by the endeavours and success of the college, the University encouraged its plans. The Principal's Report of 1926 reveals that the University Inspection Committee had recommended an increase of Rs 200 in the grant of the college.

A CURRICULUM FOR WOMEN?

From the beginning the impetus for promoting female education in India had mostly been provided by men, unlike England where women had to fight to wrest the privilege. So contentious was the struggle that even the pioneers sometimes exhibited a certain ambivalence. One uncertainty was concerning the level of education that was appropriate for women to attain. The other was with regard to the special educational needs of women, that is, the curricula.

The controversy regarding a suitable curriculum for women raged not only in colonial India but also in Victorian Britain. It is interesting to glance at the issues that were raised in Britain because similar sentiments were also expressed in Indian society. Tom Beggs in his history of Queen Margaret College of Edinburgh described the two points of view concerning subjects to be studied by women. A survey, taken during 1864 and 1867, found that teaching girls separately had resulted in a dismal state of education. Emily Davies represented the faction who believed that 'courses and examinations undertaken by women should be identical to those followed by male students'. She was afraid that 'any form of dilution of education offered to women would damage the pursuit of equality'. There were others who professed a different view, such as Anne Clough. They believed that 'educational programs might be specifically geared to perceived need for women'.[13]

In India, from the beginning, texts which women were supposed to read were carefully screened. Consequently, Sambuddha Chakrabarty finds ironical the early nineteenth-century accusation that education would wean women away from religion. Women's texts in vernacular were all native texts completely free of western influence.[14]

Exploring the pattern in India, Karuna Chanana writes that by 1882 there was considerable public opinion in favour of a differentiated curriculum. The Educational Commission of 1882 supported this view while advising a cautious approach. Chanana avers that the debate was the outcome of the fixing of rules for grants-in-aid. This grant was the mainstay of private initiatives in education. The policy did not allow innovation in education. Private schools whether run by missionaries or reformers, had to include subjects suited to girls in their curricula.[15]

To illustrate the controversy over curricula, we may take the example of Madras Presidency, a considerably progressive region as compared to the other regions of India in the early twentieth century. Padmini Swaminathan analyses the two ideas relating to secondary education in Madras Presidency prevalent in 1919. One was that girls ought to be brought up on lines as similar as possible to those laid down for boys to prepare them for a University career. The second was that girls ought to be prepared for home life and educated in all that concerned enlightened mothering and a good standard of maternal physique. It was the second view that predominated. When the Government set up an intermediate college for women, the women could only choose from among the arts course for their optional courses. Any attempt to take science subjects was considered impractical owing to the absence of laboratories. Science subjects were moreover regarded as difficult for girls. The girls' families at times had a different view regarding the efficacy of the alternative course for girls prescribed by the Government. Parents were not convinced that the value of a course that did not lead to the acquisition of a recognized certificate justified the heavy expenditure entailed in the form of school and boarding fees.[16] Their concerns however met with little response.

As late as 1927, when a conference was held in Poona by the All India Women's Conference to comprehensively discuss the subject of education of women in India, we find the 'segregationist view' persisting. The conference passed a resolution demanding separate provision of examinations and different or easier subjects for women. They propagated the view that education for homemaking was crucial. So strong was their conviction, that in 1932, Lady Irwin College was established in Delhi to teach Home Science. Lady Irwin College thereby became the third women's college in Delhi after Lady Hardinge and Indraprastha College. It is an interesting irony of history that the spearheading Indian women's organization, All India Women's Conference should have set up an institution which promoted what in feminist studies would be termed 'gender typing'. The setting up of Lady Irwin College for the express purpose of imparting 'education for homemaking' seems to point to Delhi society of the 1930s still favouring women trained to be ideal wives and mothers rather than women as serious pursuants of science and economics.[17]

However, the heartening fact was that national leaders like Nehru were opposed to this kind of essentialist thinking. In 1928, invited to lay the foundation for a woman's college in Allahabad, Nehru discovered that the college prospectus laid down that a woman's place was in the home. He criticized these ideals and observed, 'May I say that I do not agree with this idea of women's life or education. The future of India cannot consist of dolls or playthings and if you make half the population of a country the mere playthings of the other half, an encumbrance on others, how will you ever make progress?'[18]

Indraprastha College skirted this whole contentious issue and from the beginning prescribed for its students a rational mix of subjects. There were five languages—Hindi, Bengali, Urdu, English, and later Punjabi. There were the homemaking subjects—needlework, health, hygiene, and domestic science. But equal stress was laid on history, mathematics, and science. In 1928, economics was added as a subject and a few years later philosophy. And in spite of financial stringency, Indraprastha College set up laboratories signifying, that the institution did not subscribe to the essentialist view that science was difficult or unsuitable for women. However, when the college moved to Civil Lines, the science laboratories were left behind in the school building. For a long time, the governing body of the college kept alive their dream of starting science classes. In 1939 they sought grants-in-aid from the Government to start science classes. Dr B.D. Laroia, Dean of the Science Faculty in Delhi University, was welcomed as a member of the Governing Body in 1938 in the hope that when science classes were started in the college, he would guide their development. From a letter (May 1938) of the Secretary to Ex-principal Leonara G'Meiner, we learn that the Delhi University Inspection Committee visited the college in connection with the application for permission to start science classes. But the college could not comply with the minimum requirements of staff, equipment, finance, or accommodation and could not, therefore, become a science college. (For more details see Ch. 3)

INDRAPRASTHA COLLEGE: EXPANSION VS ACCOMMODATION

By 1931, Indraprastha College was facing both a resource crunch and space shortage. The problem of accommodation had become acute since the existing area also served as a hostel for the students. In 1926, there were 25 boarders from both the school and the college. Two tin sheds were constructed on the top of the building for the students to sleep during the rainy season. In summer these rooms were very hot. It was becoming urgent to move the college classes to another location. At this time of deficit, the school that was the germ of the college continued to be supportive. The students performed the play *Singhal Vijay* for the public to raise funds. Madan Theatres Ltd. of Calcutta allowed their theatre to be used and also helped by lending their scenery and staff. This is to be seen as an example of the considerable amount of goodwill that the institution had garnered in the city. The sum that was raised was earmarked for the development of the library. The fact that a public performance could be organized by this institution is in itself a great indicator of changes in north Indian society.[19]

The space constraint in the old Delhi building led the authorities of the college to cast around for a building to move into. By 1928, the founders had seen a gleam of hope—it was from this year that the first mention of Alipur House is encountered in the annual reports of the college.[20] In a letter to the Managing Member of the school and college, the Superintendent of Education, Delhi, Ajmer, Mewar, promised that the Government of India would give the first refusal of the Alipur House to the college, whenever the property was available for disposal. The assurances of the Government notwithstanding, the college had to struggle for a decade before it could acquire the building (see Chapter 3). The fact that Alipur House was near the University made it an attractive site to both Indraprastha and Lady Irwin College.

The year 1932 was a kind of anus mirabulis for the college. It was in this year that Indraprastha College leased Chandrawali Bhawan, a bungalow in Civil Lines. The house was made available through the generosity of Piyarelal Motorwale, who had in the past donated two buses to the school. Families from the old city of Delhi had been moving to the Civil Lines for several decades. According to Sheila Dhar, these new inhabitants of the Civil Lines were like her grandfather, loyalist officers of the Raj.[21] Eventually daughters of these families came to study at Indraprastha College.

The school remained in the old building, in the house donated by Lala Balkrishan Das. By moving to the Civil Lines, Indraprastha College had moved close to Alipur House, as well as near the University. At Chandrawali Bhawan, there was more space for the college students. The college boarders could also live here. Leonara G'meiner continued to be the Principal of both the school and the college. The rent of the building was fixed at Rs 175. The necessity to pay rent for the college building separately resulted in a deficit in the finances of the college. A separate establishment and separate additional staff meant additional expenditure.

However, the move to Chandrawali Bhawan facilitated the movement of Indraprastha students to the University colleges for their undergraduate classes. F.F. Monk in his history of St. Stephen's College noted that since intermediate classes were started for women at Indraprastha College, the BA classes at St. Stephen's College were proving to be quite full. At times there were as many as ten women in a class.[22] From the reminiscences of the students of those times who had done their intermediate at Indraprastha College, such as the writer Chandra Rajan, one learns that even at St. Stephen's College, a strict supervision was maintained over the female pupils. They were escorted to their mixed classes and escorted back to the ladies common room at the end of the class. Society was still deeply protective about women.

That year, a third-year class was started to follow the intermediate classes at Indraprastha College. There were 59 students in the three classes. Another landmark of the year was that the University granted permission to women students to sit privately for examinations, fulfilling one of the demands of the AIWC in 1927, at its historic meeting in Poona.

By 1932, the college had initiated steps towards the introduction of degree classes. The Governing Body at its meeting on 12 November, 1932 passed a resolution to apply for recognition of degree classes. The college was required to satisfy the authorities regarding the subjects taught, accommodation, library, exact qualifications, and experience of the staff and ensure that none of the college teachers were teaching in Indraprastha School. For this it was necessary to separate the school and college bodies. Thus a separate Board of

Trustees was formed for the college. Physical separation by location was now followed by a formal disjunction. The move from Chhipiwara to Civil Lines was now complete. Indraprastha School and Indraprastha College became distinct bodies.

THE VISITORS' BOOK REVEALS

Many distinguished personalities visited the institution between the years 1924 and 1932. Both high representatives of the Raj and fervent nationalists have recorded their impressions in the visitors' book. The comments enforce the impressions of a complex experiment in 'inventing' modern Indian womanhood being attempted in Indraprastha College.

The 1927 visitors' book reveals that the Chief Commissioner's wife as well as Meerabai from the Satyagraha Ashram at Sabarmati visited the school that year. On 10 February, 1928, the vicerine Lady Irwin had paid a royal visit to Indraprastha College. On one occasion during the vicerine Lady Irwin's visit to the school, when Leonara G'meiner escorted the vicerine to the interior of the school, the retinue as well as the large gathering of Delhi citizens had to be left behind in the front courtyard. This indicates the rigid enforcement of the *purdah* restrictions. Running a women's institution in the early twentieth century was not an easy responsibility. Any infringement of the privacy and protection of the inmates was regarded with disapprobation by the conservative society. In the writings of Rokeya Sakhawat Hossain (1880–1932), the Calcutta educationist and social reformer, who ran a school for Muslim girls in Calcutta from 1911, there are hilarious descriptions of the predicament that she had to face due to the extreme sensitivity of her community with regard to *purdah*.[23]

In 1929, Annie Besant visited the school and the college for the second time. She wrote, 'This school trains the Indian women as citizen as well as a wife and a mother.' This was in continuity with her views in the influential essay on education of Indian women, as referred to in the first chapter, though the inclusion of the word citizen was welcome. The comment reflects twin ideals, the cause of Indian Home Rule and the recovery of ancient values of Indian civilization. In tune with the vision of Annie Besant, the college instituted the Sitaram Scholarship for the 'best student' of class IV in 1929.

In 1930, Sarojini Naidu, who was deeply interested in the issue of women's education, visited the school and penned a poetic line about 'the blossoming of the school'. Another visitor that year was Rai Harbilas Sarda, who is associated with an important legislation concerning the lives of Indian women. Sarda had campaigned for prohibiting child marriage and was instrumental in having a law passed to prohibit it. He was in the tradition of the long line of reformers such as Vidyasagar. Sarda wrote in the visitor's book: 'The girls imbibe here good traditions of Indian society and will make useful members of that society.' Once again the emphasis on society rather than just the family was heartening.

In April 1930, V.J. Patel, President of the Legislative Assembly, inscribed the following message in the visitor's book: 'I am very pleased to visit this institution and wish it every success. I am sure that the Principal will not misunderstand me if I say that the use of foreign cloth should be strictly prohibited in this institution which is otherwise an ideal one.' However, despite the exhortations of V.J. Patel, the Principal did not make the wearing of *khadi* compulsory for the students. Coercion was out of question. The use of *khadi* had to be inspired by example. As an incentive, therefore, a prize was instituted for the student who donned the best dress in *khadi*.

Notes and References

1. Aparna Basu, 'A Century's Journey: Women's Education in Western India, 1820–1920', in Karuna Chanana (ed.), *Socialization, Education and Women: Exploration of Gender Identity*, Orient Longman, New Delhi, 1988, p. 83.

2. 'Indraprastha Girls School and College', *Chand*, September 1929.

3. Ibid.

4. Kumari Jayawardene, *Feminism and Nationalism in the Third World*, Kali for Women, New Delhi, 1986, p. 89.

5. Michelle Maskiell, *Women Between Cultures*, p. 14.

6. Padmini Swaminathan, 'Women's Education in Colonial Tamilnadu, 1900–30: The Coalescence of Patriarchy and Colonialism', in *Indian Journal of Gender Studies*, July 1999, p. 28.

7. Ibid., p. 30.

8. Rama Mehta, *The Western Educated Hindu Women*, Asia Publishing House, 1970, p. 25

9. Padmini Swaminathan, 'Women's Education in Colonial Tamilnadu, 1900–30', p. 30.

10. Michelle Maskiell, *Women Between Cultures*, p. 158.

11. Aparna Basu, 'A Century's Journey', p. 71.

12. Sucheta Kripalani was a prominent Congress worker and one of the few women who were elevated to the position of Chief Minister of UP and then as Governor of UP.

13. Tom Beggs, *The Excellent Women: The Origin and History of Queen Margaret College*, John Donald, Edinburgh, 1994, p. 13.

14. Sambuddha Chakrabarty, *Antare Andare*, p. 59.

15. Karuna Chanana, 'Social Change or Social Reform: The Education of Women in Pre-independence India', in Karuna Chanana (ed.), *Socialization, Women and Education*, p. 117.

16. Padmini Swaminathan, 'Women's Education in Colonial Tamilnadu, 1900–30', p. 35.

17. As time passed, Lady Irwin College did not remain limited to the teaching of Home Science. It now imparts education in valuable scientific fields such as nutrition and child psychology, to mention only two among many.

18. Padmini Swaminathan, 'Women's Education in Colonial Tamilnadu, 1900–30, p. 35.

19. In earlier years, there are indications that one Principal had incurred the school secretary's displeasure at having countenanced the participation of the students in a function arranged by Ramjas College.

20. Alipur House was a colonial style building built in 1917–18. In 1928, there were still 16 European families of soldiers living in it. The building was the residence of the Commander-in-Chief.

21. Sheila Dhar, *Here's Someone I'd Like You To Meet*, Oxford University Press, New Delhi, p. 20.

22. F.F. Monk, *History of St. Stephens College*, YMCA Press, Calcutta, 1935, p. 222.

23. Rokeya Sakhawat Hossain, 'Abarodhbasini', in Abdul Qadir (ed.), *Rokeya Rachanabali*, Bangla Academy, Dacca, 1984, p. 86.

1. Speeches of Mahatma Gandhi at [illegible] as per [illegible] measure of the few women who were relevant to the [illegible] of Gandhi Mahatma of 1930 and thereof [illegible] 1969 p. 7.

12. Tara Devi [illegible] [illegible] from a interview after Quoting Congress Morarji Desai; also Joint Gandhi's in February 1969 p. 5.

13. Sucheta Kripalani, [illegible] ibid; Jowar History, p. 5.

14. Aruna Ghimiry [illegible] from [illegible] for Social Reform, the Eli role of Women in the independence India on Kamala Channar roll', Young Generation Women and Politics p. 212.

15. Hiramati ahead 'Women's Education in Colonial Traditional [illegible]

3

The Shaping of the Young Women
of a Growing City, 1933–39

The 1930s were politically and economically significant in the history of India as well as the world. The 1929 economic depression in the USA affected the economy of the entire world, as the steep decline in production and foreign trade resulted in large-scale unemployment and economic distress. The Depression discredited the capitalist system, leading to the growth of socialist ideas. And then came the Second World War in 1939.

The economic depression that encapsulated the entire world adversely affected the conditions of the peasants and workers in India as well. The prices of agricultural products dropped by over 50% per cent by the end of 1932. The employers threatened reduction of wages. The peasants, throughout the country, demanded land reforms, abolition of zamindari, reduction of land revenue and rent, and relief from indebtedness. The factory and plantation workers, on the other hand, demanded better conditions of work and recognition of their trade union rights. The mobilization of the workers and the peasants led to the growth of trade unions and *kisan sabhas* in several parts of India, particularly Uttar Pradesh, Bihar, Andhra Pradesh, Tamil Nadu, Kerala, and Punjab. Incidents such as the shooting of cotton textile workers in Bombay who went on strike to demand a better socio-economic status, alienated the people even more and spurred them on in their resistance against the British authorities. The national struggle in the 1930s was thus closely associated with and influenced by the political and economic events in the rest of the world.

The Civil Disobedience Movement engulfed the entire nation during this period.

SOCIAL AND BEHAVIORAL RESPONSES OF WOMEN TO THE NATIONAL MOVEMENT

There is no doubt that the social, economic, and political developments of the 1930s had a deep impact on the minds and attitudes of Indian youth. A review of the responses and reactions of the students of Indraprastha College will provide an idea of the influence of these development on young minds, particularly young women.

The political activities in Indraprastha College and its critical responses to government policies took different forms in the course of the national struggle. One such expression was the boycott of the visit of Vicerine Doreen Linlithgow to the college in 1937. It may be reiterated that this was a period when the college authorities were locked in a dialogue with the Government for the acquisition of a larger building for the college and government grants to facilitate the purchase of such a building. These exigencies notwithstanding, the students stood adamantly opposed to any representation of British authority. What was remarkable, particularly in the given circumstances, was that neither the teachers nor the college management dissuaded the students from their deep interest or involvement in national politics or discouraged their resistance. While the management or the teachers never incited the students, they also neither interfered in nor banned their activities.

It would be interesting to note the students' reactions and responses to the Congress session at Lahore in 1929 and the Second Civil Disobedience Movement launched by Gandhi in March 1930. The Congress, at Lahore, passed a resolution declaring that *Poorna Swaraj* (absolute freedom) was its objective and in pursuance of this declaration, the tricolour flag of freedom was hoisted on 31 December, 1929. Twenty-sixth of January 1930 was fixed as the first Independence Day. It was to be celebrated every year, with the Indians taking the pledge that it was a crime against man and God to submit any longer to British rule. The Congress also announced the Second Civil Disobedience Movement. Responding to the call of the Congress and to commemorate *Poorna Swaraj*, the students of Indraprastha College celebrated January 26 as Independence Day in 1930, and did so every year since then. They hoisted the tricolour on this day, circulated the Independence Day manifesto, and took the pledge of *Azadi*.[1]

The participation of women from both rural and urban areas, in the Second Civil Disobedience Movement was phenomenal. The movement was sparked off by Gandhi's Dandi march. Women were particularly effective in picketing liquor and foreign cloth shops.[2] Their involvement was also significant in the *khadi* campaign (to wear home-spun cloth) as well as in the general political demonstrations and mass agitation.[3] That the participation of women in this movement was impressive is evident from Nehru's observations about the days of the Civil Disobedience Movement. He talked about the 'avalanche' of women during this period that took not only the British Government but also the Indian men by surprise. Women from all sections of the society—upper or middle class, leading sheltered lives in their homes, peasant women, working-class women, rich women, poor women—poured out in defiance of government orders and police *lathis*. In all their activities, Nehru said, women displayed not only courage and daring but a 'surprising' organizational power.[4]

During the Second Civil Disobedience Movement, a woman who mobilized and awakened the women of Delhi was Satyawati, granddaughter of Swami Shraddhanand. She was deeply influenced by Gandhi who had urged women to be *sabala* (strong) and the makers of their destiny. Satyawati persuaded women to come out of their homes and join the freedom struggle. Her participation in the national movement was so energetic that Gandhi affectionately called her *toofani* (storm-like).[5] Satyawati led women in Delhi to picket shops and persuade the rich women who came to bathe in the Yamuna river to abandon the use of foreign clothes.[6] A large number of women who joined Satyawati in her marches to the Yamuna were students of Indraprastha College, representing the educated women of Delhi. Responding to the call of boycott of foreign cloth, Indraprastha students in 1931 led by Chameli Devi participated in the burning—or, as it was popularly known, *holi*—of the *videshi* clothes in *kutcha* Ghasi Ram, a lane in the walled city of Delhi. Not satisfied by the general bonfire, the students organized a similar *holi* in the back verandah of Indraprastha School, where the college was situated in those days.[7]

The active involvement of Indraprastha College in the national struggle presents an interesting contrast to the reactions of St. Stephen's

College in Delhi. The Civil Disobedience Movement of 1930–31 had led to political and racial tensions in St. Stephen's College. The Students' Union of this college was against the movement despite the fact that several students of the college had participated in the *hartals* and hoisted the national flag on the flagstaff of the college. The Students' Union carried out an 'invasion' against such students who were active in the *hartals*. But the college could overcome and survive the crisis by channelling the students' energies into 'positive *swadeshi* promotion in preference to negative boycott'. The transformation in the students' attitude was achieved through the 'healthy mindedness' made possible by the 'normal scale of values' as revealed in the autumn of 1930. During this season, the students of St. Stephen's College, who had declined invitation after invitation to indulge in political *hartals*, cut lectures en masse to go and watch the English MCC team play cricket![8]

Whatever the responses of St. Stephen's College, Ramjas and Hindu College observed complete *hartal* and participated in the burning of foreign cloth. The students of Indraprastha College continued to picket liquor and foreign cloth shops and march in procession through the lanes and bylanes of Delhi—Neela Ka Katra, Ballimaran, Nai Sarak—singing patriotic songs, beating drums and raising slogans. Many of the students took to wearing *khadi*. They had learnt to weave on the *charkha* and made their own *saris* from *sut* or cotton thread. Many students, inspired by Bankim Chandra's *Anand Math*, Rabindranath Tagore's *Geetanjali* and Sarat Chandra's stories, narrated anecdotes and stories from these literary works to fellow students and to the women outside the college, to influence them into joining the national movement.[9] These activities of the students of Indraprastha College encapsulated what was happening throughout India. Whether it was Bengal, Bihar, Delhi, Gujarat, Punjab, or Karnataka, *prabhat pheris*, (processions at dawn), meetings, and picketing was becoming almost a daily routine. During the salt *satyagraha* over 80,000 persons were arrested, of whom more than 17,000 were women.[10]

The beginning of the 1930s thus marked a period of intense introspection and dilemma for the colonial government. On the one hand, it had to strategize to counter the rising national resentment against its rule and on the other, plan its survival under the impact of the economic depression and the Second World War. In an attempt to overcome these adverse circumstances, the British Government announced several financial cuts, threatened withdrawal of government grants to institutions, and became increasingly hesitant about meeting deficits or renewing subsidies to educational institutions. Although the Government attitude created problems for all educational institutions, it particularly affected women's colleges such as Indraprastha, which were actively engaged in spreading and popularizing education amongst women.

INDRAPRASTHA COLLEGE: PROBLEMS OF 'SPACE' IN THE MIDST OF NATIONAL ACTIVITIES

In its various phases of growth, Indraprastha College was closely intertwined with the changing character of Delhi. Delhi in the 1930s was moving towards being a cosmopolitan city. Increasing number of Punjabis and Bengalis had come to the city, though many of its original inhabitants insisted on retaining their different sense of being and their general indifference to national politics.[11] The growing cosmopolitan population of Delhi, particularly the Punjabis and Bengalis (who had much earlier been exposed to modern education), emphasized the need for higher education for their sons and daughters. For the girls, Lady Irwin College was established in 1932 in Delhi to teach Home Science. But it was not affiliated to Delhi University and neither were its standards considered very high. In fact, it was often being asked what could the girls learn in this college that they could not learn at home.[12] Then, there was Lady Hardinge Medical College (established in 1916 in Delhi) which imparted knowledge in medical science to women. However Indraprastha College remained the only stepping stone for girls keen on pursuing a BA degree in liberal arts in Delhi. It was the only women's college in Delhi, recognized by Delhi University, that offered intermediate classes in Humanities and Social Sciences. Therefore, girls seeking higher education made a bee-line for this institution.

The increasing number of students made the college authorities even more conscious of the constraints of physical space. Since 1924, when the intermediate classes were introduced, the college had been housed in the two rooms of Indraprastha School, situated near Jama Masjid. Over the years, as more women sought admission, the need arose for more space. In the absence of any financial support, tin sheds were put up on the roof of the school to create more classrooms and hostel rooms. Such tin and iron structures must have caused tremendous hardships for the students, particularly during the summer months and the rainy season. But their desire for education was so strong that they were willing to put up with such dismal accommodation. With the continuous increase in the number of students, the college authorities often feared that the prevailing circumstances might compel them to stop new admissions. From 1931 onwards the college management began an even more desperate hunt for a larger building.

Leonara G'meiner had initiated the search for a larger building for the college as early as 1926. She zeroed in on Alipur House, the office of the Commander-in-Chief, as the ideal location. The Government expressed its willingness to consider the idea, yet for almost a decade there were only negotiations for the acquisition of Alipur House. The history of the college's attempts to acquire Alipur House is detailed in a subsequent subsection.

Leonara G'meiner, despite her sincere endeavours had failed to convince the British Government of the necessity of the prompt release of Alipur House. By 1931, with the rapid increase in the number of students, a larger building had become imperative. This problematic legacy was inherited by Kalavati Gupta, who assumed office as the Principal of the college in 1931 after Leonara G'meiner's retirement.

THE COLLEGE IN THE PRECINCTS OF CHANDRAWALI BHAWAN

Reacting to the growing severity of accommodation, one of the benefactors of the college, Lala Piyare Lal Motorwale, offered to lease his *kothi* (bungalow) called Chandrawali Bhawan to the college. This bungalow belonged to the Asharfi Devi and Chandrawali Devi Trusts created by Lala Piyare Lal in the memory of his two wives. To begin with, Indraprastha School was the beneficiary of the two trusts. These trusts were instituted in 1925 for the promotion of women's education in Delhi. At first, Motorwale had given *mauza* (village) Asalatpur in district Meerut to provide revenue for running the two charitable trusts. In 1927, on the request of the school authorities, he gave one of his bungalows in exchange for the village. It was to this bungalow that the college moved in 1931. The renting of Chandrawali Bhawan incurred a huge expenditure for the college. In addition to the house rent of Rs 175, the governing body of the college had to engage separate teaching and non-teaching staff for the college. Moreover, to provide sufficient teaching work to the college teachers, it became obligatory for the college to introduce three-year classes, that is, one year of FA (Fine Arts).[13] In fact, the admissions of 1932 show an increasing number of students—the significant feature of which was that apart from Hindu girls, a large number of the Muslim and Christian girls also sought admission. Increasing numbers and a cosmopolitan atmosphere have characterized Indraprastha College since the 1930s.

Chandrawali Bhawan, situated in Civil Lines, was a double-storied, inter-connected bungalow with high walls that accommodated both the college and the hostel. The surroundings of the bungalow were unlike a college campus—the compound was not spacious enough to provide playgrounds or lawns or open fields. However, the impressions of Monta Bose, a student of the college in 1931–33, are different. She remembers Chandrawali Bhawan as being spacious, with lovely lawns and flowering shrubs and trees. 'It was a welcome change after the cramped existence in the school building.'[14] The college began to develop sports facilities like netball and badminton courts along the terraced gardens of Chandrawali Bhawan. Basket ball and volleyball were two other sports the students could now try out their hand at. Apart from sports, the college also strove to enhance the extra-curricular potentialities of its students by encouraging them to participate in inter-college activities such as debate and music competitions. The students of Indraprastha College competed with their male counterparts on equal terms. The students of the 1930s remember with pride how they lifted inter-college debate trophies in competition with colleges such as St. Stephen's.

In 1933–34, when the college had shifted to Chandrawali Bhawan, Girl Guides, pioneered and introduced by Baden-Powell, was a popular activity of the college. The Girl Guides Company of the college was called Number 4 Delhi Company. Many girls from this Company, without any teacher escorting them, attended Miss Garson's camp at Badli in Delhi in 1934.[15] The purpose of Girl Guides was to instill confidence and develop the personality of the girl-students. But it had yet another aim—to arouse support and awe for British imperialism and the British monarch. One of the exercises that the Government had ordered for the Girl Guides was to salute the Union Jack and shout slogans such as 'Long live the King', 'God save the King, Long live to rule over us'. But the Girl Guides of Indraprastha College, imbued with nationalistic fervour, defied government orders. In 1933–34, they formed a group called Zinnia Patrol which refused to salute the Union Jack and replaced the official slogan by 'God save everybody, Go away from us'. The Zinnia Patrol displeased the authorities of the Girl Guides by their disrespect to the British monarchy. The authorities threatened severe action against these students of the college. Leonara G'meiner intervened to prevent any drastic consequences and appealed to the *zinnia patrol* to abandon its resistance. Unmoved and undaunted, the patrol remained adamant and refused to either salute the British flag or sing or chant slogans in praise of the British King. It is worthwhile to note that despite the unyielding behaviour of the students on one hand and the threats of the Girl Guides authorities on the other, Leonara G'meiner took no action against these students.[16]

It was in the midst of such defiance and courage that the students of Indraprastha College were moulded. The students were also inspired by the visits of politically active women such as Sarojini Naidu and Satyawati to the college.[17] Whenever Gandhi or Nehru came to the vicinity of the college, the girls did not hesitate to violate college regulations to see them or listen to their speeches. The excitement about meeting national heroes was so high that the students sometimes even jumped the college walls apart from cutting lectures.[18] Inspired by Gandhi's message to fight the caste system and the fact that he stayed in the Harijan *basti* situated in the neighbourhood of Chandrawali Bhawan, the students made it a practice to visit this *basti* regularly. Breaking their family and social taboos, the girls taught the *basti* inhabitants the importance of health, hygiene, and science. The students also taught the *basti* children in the college premises during their free periods.[19]

In the mid-1930s, the Congress proposed training for girls in self-defence, to teach them defence tactics in case the British attacked. The lessons were in the use of hands or fists and, at the most, *lathi*. In view of Gandhi's determination to practice *ahimsa*, training in the art of revolvers, and such other weapons was unthinkable. For the years 1936–38, a student of Indraprastha College, Sarla Sharma was made the commander of the group of girls in Delhi who volunteered to take lessons in self-defence.[20] During this period, the Congress also organized protests against the massacre of 1919 at Jalianwala Bagh, to demonstrate that the anger of the people had not waned. The protest march was taken out in Chandni Chowk in Delhi. Nearly five thousand women, including a large number of students from Indraprastha College, dressed in white *khadi,* marched in the procession raising slogans against British arbitrariness and tyranny and singing

Nahi Rakhni Nahi Rakhni, Zalim Sarkar Nahi Rakhni
Jalianwala Bagh Me Jakar Nihatha Mari
Nahi Rakhni Nahi Rakhni ...[21]

The strength and enthusiasm of women during this period was boundless as they joined their male counterparts in the national movement to weaken and ultimately shake the base of British imperialism.

TOWARDS A NEW IDENTITY

As noted in chapter 2, the distinct identity of the college, separate from that of Indraprastha School, was firmly established by early 1932, when the management of the college was entrusted to a separate Board of Trustees and Governing Body. From 1932 onwards, the college became an independent unit. The college authorities, during this period, with the intention of expanding the facilities in college, contemplated a fourth-year degree class to enable the third-year students to continue their studies in the college. Till 1932, in the absence of any provision for degree classes in the college, the girls had to join co-educational colleges for further studies. In such circumstances, conservative families, hesitant to send their daughters to co-educational institutions, withdrew their daughters from studies after FA, putting an end to their educational career. The intended fourth-year degree class thus offered a great hope for the aspiring young women.

The governing body of the college had, since 1932, sought to impress upon the Government the need for a degree college exclusively for women, making persistent appeals for elevating Indraprastha College to a degree college. The vice chancellor of Delhi University, Professor M. Abdur Rahman, had also stressed the necessity for a degree college for women in his convocation address of 1931. He pointed out that in the absence of an exclusive degree college for women, they were 'compelled to attend lectures in men's colleges'. He conceded that men's colleges provided special facilities for women students, yet these students could never 'completely benefit from college life' since they could not 'feel free to groom themselves according to their own special requirements'. The vice chancellor reiterated that if the education of women had to move beyond formal instructions in the classrooms and provide women with an independent status in the society, it was necessary to establish a degree college for women in Delhi. He regretted that a large number of women in Delhi had to go elsewhere for further studies after passing their intermediate examination from Delhi University. The governing body derived much encouragement from the vice chancellor's words, to press for the derived introduction of degree classes in the college.[22]

However, even as the college made claims for its elevation to a degree college, it found itself in dire financial straits. To overcome the mounting deficits, the college was compelled to depend upon the small endowment fund of Rs 50,000 allotted for maintaining the intermediate classes. The college already owed the bank a credit of Rs 10,000, and it was realized that further expansion of the college would add a sum of Rs 9000 to the deficit. In such circumstances, it appealed to the philanthropists of Delhi for donations and support to build an endowment fund of one lakh rupees for its maintenance and expansion. The college authorities also appealed for government funds. Meanwhile, they applied to the University for raising the status of the college to a degree college. In response, the University of Delhi appointed a commission to ascertain whether the demand of the college could be fulfilled. The members of the commission visited the college in March 1933. Ignoring the pioneering efforts of the college towards women's education, it refused to recommend the college as a degree college to the Academic Council of the University, citing reasons such as its budget deficits, and no definite assurance of a government grant or public donations.

The two aspirations of Indraprastha College—the recognition as a degree college and the acquisition of Alipur House—seemed beyond reach in the face of its enormous financial crisis. The recurring and non-recurring deficits were so exorbitant that the management at one point even considered closing down the college. Such contemplation on the part of this premier educational institution for girls sent shock waves throughout Delhi, as evident from a report in a leading newspaper published from Delhi. It was reported that unless adequate funds were available or unless the Government came to its rescue, there was little possibility of the college being able to sustain itself.[23]

Focused on the objective of tiding over the financial problems, the college set up an educational committee. One of its purposes was to win the Support of the educational commissioner and to persuade the Superintendent of Education to make an extra grant of Rs 5000 to the college. The Education Department, despite the appeals of the educational committee, remained unrelenting on the issue of additional grants or any other financial aid to the college. Faced with the dubious reactions of the Government and rare hopes of donations from the public, the educational committee of the college, much to its chagrin, was compelled to recommend the closure of the college after the existing second-and fourth-year classes had appeared for the University examinations in April 1935.

The recommendation of the educational committee to close the college in view of the financial scarcities was obviously not a pleasant decision for the trustees of the college. Not keen to implement it, they closeted themselves for further discussions to tide over the crisis. The trustees were hopeful that since the educational policy of the University and the Government regarding higher education was under consideration, it may in the course of its evolution promote the interests of the college and develop its resources. They were also apprehensive about the legality of the resolution to close the college. While the college management continued its deliberations, Lala Shankar Lal of Delhi Cloth Mill emerged as a saviour. In April 1934, he offered a donation sufficient to facilitate the functioning of the college for at least another year. His philanthropy could thus defer the closing of the college by one year. Revived once again, the college launched upon its usual exercise of admitting students to first-and third-year classes. Keeping the college alive under such circumstances was a difficult task for the governing body of the college and it again renewed its appeal to the Government for a grant. But before the Government could respond, a newspaper report summed up the intentions of the Government. It reported that the Government could contemplate financial assistance to the college only if certain terms and conditions were fulfilled, seeking to confirm the rampant rumour that the Government had asked the college to completely overhaul its policies and administration as a pre-condition for government support.[24] Repudiating such reports, the Principal and the honorary secretary of the college committee, in a letter to the editor of *The Hindustan Times*, accused the newspaper of supporting rumours that cast aspersions on the image of the college. They denied any government demand for the overhaul of the policies or the administration of the college and attributed the Government's tough attitude to 'not over-friendly feelings towards the institution'.[25]

Despite its perennial financial problems, in its first ten years of existence, the college had shown remarkable progress both in terms of its results and its expanding popularity. In 1934, it sent 7 students as private candidates for the BA examination since the college was not yet equipped as a degree college. Seventeen students appeared for the intermediate examination, all of whom had acquitted themselves creditably. It had aroused tremendous trust and confidence amongst the people of Delhi. Being the only women's college in Delhi, it also generated an exceptionally kind and sympathetic response from the principals and the teachers of the other colleges of Delhi. By 1934–35, it attracted students from all sections of the society irrespective of caste or religious faith: while it had registered only 5 students in 1924, by 1934–35, the number had gone up to 71, of which nine were Muslims and two Christian. As the college grew and its student body became more and more cosmopolitan, the college management contemplated approaching an experienced Muslim educationist to be a member of the its governing body. The attempt was probably to emphasize the secular credentials of the institution and tone down its 'Hindu' character, something it had often been accused of possessing.

YET ANOTHER CONTROVERSY

Even as Indraprastha College endeavoured to grow and strengthen its roots, there were misleading representations about the nature of the college by a section of the Delhi public. These allegations were the outcome of the growing communal tension in the country, engendered by the British Government. The Government had aroused separatist sentiments by proposing elections for the legislative assemblies on the basis of restricted franchise and separate electorates. By its manoeuvres, the Government had succeeded in breaking the unity of the Congress and the Muslim League. Initially united on the common ground of ousting the British from power, the Congress and the Muslim League had become increasingly suspicious of each other. Reconciliation between the two seemed unlikely. The Muslim League issued a statement that the Muslim minority was in danger of being engulfed by the Hindu majority. The Delhi Muslim Association appeared to have imbibed these sentiments. The Association expressed apprehensions, similar to that of the Muslim League, through a deputation to the Viceroy of India. It urged the Viceroy to provide special patronage to the Muslims of Delhi, who were a 'backward and a poor community' and whose 'needs were many'.[26] The

Association complained that while for the Muslim boys there was only one college—the Anglo-Arabic college, maintained by the Itmad-ud-daulah Trust for over a century—the 'majority community' had three colleges in Delhi—Ramjas, Hindu and St. Stephen's. It also observed that while these colleges received building grants from the Government, the Anglo-Arabic College was not a beneficiary of any such government support. The Association, urged the Viceroy to either sanction a special grant to the Anglo-Arabic College for a new building on the University site or get a new building constructed for the college by the Public Works Department (PWD). The Delhi Muslim Association's demands for financial support and a building grant were undoubtedly valid. But the issue became complicated and communal when they talked about the education of Muslim women, misconstruing the nature of Indraprastha College and nurturing false apprehensions about it. The Association alleged that while there were several girls' high schools and a girls' college (the reference was obviously to Indraprastha College) maintained by the Hindus, no such institutions existed for Muslim girls. It argued that though the Government had offered to maintain a university college for women in Delhi, the Executive Council of the University supported the claims of the 'Hindu' Girls' College (the reference was again to Indraprastha College).[27] But, as the history of the college illustrates, it was far from being 'Hindu' in its approach or character, despite the fact that except for two members on its Governing Body—C.B. Young, a Christian, and Dr Zakir Hussain, a Muslim—the rest of the members were Hindus. Harbouring a variety of such misgivings and fears, the Association expressed its doubts about the implementation of the scheme for a federal University in Delhi. It apprehended that the scheme would give a monopoly to the existing 'Hindu' Girls' College for higher education for women. Appealing on behalf of the Muslims of Delhi, the Association urged the Viceroy, who was also the Chancellor of Delhi University, to favour a non-denominational university college for women in Delhi.[28]

The Viceroy, playing to the communal mood of the nation and perhaps abetting it, sympathized with the allegations of the Delhi Muslim Association without investigating the charges against the so-called 'Hindu' Girls' college, that is, Indraprastha College. He, however, did concede that Indraprastha College had persistently appealed to the University to devise a plan for the development of higher education for all women, caste and community notwithstanding. The Viceroy understood the true character of Indraprastha College, but for strategic reasons, made no attempt to remove the misunderstandings of the Delhi Muslim Association. Instead, to silence the opposition of the Association to the Government, he sought its support. The Viceroy declared that the Government would not recognize Indraprastha College as the university college for women and that in all matters of university education for girls, the interests of all communities would be the concern of the Government.[29] The apprehensions of some sections of Muslims in Delhi and the Government regarding Indraprastha College seem unfounded. The college, on no occasion, had raised contentious issues relating to caste or religion. On the contrary, each student enjoyed the fundamental liberty to religious freedom. This distinguishing characteristic of Indraprastha College had motivated many families—Hindus, Muslims, and Christians—to send their women here to study without any fear of losing their values, principles, or identity.

A Degree College

The travails of the college continued, particularly with regard to funds, recognition of degree classes by the University, and the acquisition of Alipur House. The government decision on these matters had been pending since 1926. Regretting the behaviour of the Government, Leonara G'meiner (who even after her retirement had maintained a link with the college), in a letter to the honorary secretary Lala Jugal Kishore, accused the Government of political and social bias and held it responsible for the adversities in the college: 'the Government had treated the 'Hindu' colleges very badly. Now that so many Congress members are in the legislative assembly and form a large part of the Government, can they not do something to help a 'Hindu' institution?'[30] The use of the term 'Hindu' was evidently in order to distinguish Indraprastha College from the missionary colleges. Perhaps the strong cosmopolitan, nationalist, and cohesive character of the college perturbed the Government. It can be conjectured that the Government's rigid stand on the financial grants and the release of Alipur House could have been motivated by the objective of taking over the college and controlling its policies and decisions.

In the midst of these controversies, the Academic Council of Delhi University took a bold decision in November 1936. Reiterating its faith in Indraprastha College in promoting higher education amongst women of all castes and creed, not only from Delhi but also from different parts of India, it recommended the recognition of the college to the Executive Council, the highest decision-making body of the University. By 1937, the Executive Council of Delhi University was willing to consider the recognition of the college as a degree college. However, it insisted that the final decision would have to await the reorganization of University education. Fearing that this argument could be a tactical move to either delay or refuse recognition, the college management argued that the reorientation or restructuring of University education could not be a ground for refusing recognition to a college that was already a recognized intermediate college of the University. It was reiterated that Indraprastha College should be treated at par with the other colleges in any system of reorganization, that is, the same procedure that was adopted with regard to the recognition of the other intermediate colleges as degree colleges ought to be followed in this instance also, albeit Indraprastha College, being the only women's college in Delhi for higher education, deserved a more liberal and an appreciative treatment.

The University of Delhi finally recognized the college as a degree college in July 1937. Along with Indraprastha College, several other colleges were also recognized as colleges of the University—St. Stephen's, Hindu, Ramjas, Anglo-Arabic and Commercial College. Recognized as a degree college, Indraprastha College could now provide instruction up to BA (Pass) in English with a vernacular language, Economics, History, Mathematics, Philosophy, Sanskrit, Hindi, Urdu, and Bengali. The Board of Trustees of Indraprastha College was advised to reconstitute the governing body in such a way so as to include a sufficient ratio of representatives from communities other than Hindus as well. It was also stipulated that any one member of the teaching staff should be nominated as a representative on the governing body. The governing body was also entrusted with the responsibility of general administration of the college and interaction with the authorities of Delhi University. As a step towards strengthening the ties of affiliation with the University, the teachers of the college were obliged to sign a form of agreement with the University. The most perplexing condition, in return for recognition, was the replacement of all men teachers by women teachers and the insistence that no male teachers would be appointed in future by the college. This directive, on the basis of circumstantial evidence, does not appear to be an attempt at gender isolation since men teachers had been employed in Indraprastha College since its inception. The reason ostensibly seemed to be a desire to cut the expenditure on the salaries of the teachers. Women teachers, in those days, were paid less than men teachers. It took several years of struggle for the recognition of gender equality in the teaching profession in the University of Delhi.

ALIPUR HOUSE AND INDRAPRASTHA COLLEGE: THE HISTORY

The recognition of degree classes was a landmark in the evolution of Indraprastha College. Girls no longer had to plead with their parents to permit them to attend co-educational colleges to complete their studies or appear privately for BA examinations. Thus, more and more girls sought admission to Indraprastha College. Chandrawali Bhawan began to burst in its seams by 1937. Many a time, admissions were refused because of the lack of accommodation. From its early years, Indraprastha College had spread its wings much beyond Delhi. The number of students from outside Delhi kept on increasing, resulting in overwhelming pressure on the hostel accommodation.

Kalavati Gupta, the Principal and the college management awaited even more eagerly the sale of Alipur House by the Government. As noted above, efforts to acquire Alipur House were initiated by Leonara G'meiner as early as 1925. Since the early years of the establishment of the college, she was determined to move it from its narrow confines in Chhipiwara (north-west corner of Jama Masjid) to the open spaces of the Civil Lines area. In her search for a new building for the college, G'meiner considered several sites and options. One of the suggestions was that since St. Stephen's College had shifted to the University (its present location), Indraprastha College could buy its old building at Kashmere Gate. In view of the space crisis, this suggestion should have been accepted. But several hurdles remained—it was within the city walls, the space did not seem adequate, there were no playgrounds and above all, it was across the street from Hindu College, a co-educational college. Eventually, she earmarked Alipur House with its spacious grounds, situated near Metcalfe House on Alipur Road.

Alipur House, in 1925, was being used as a temporary residence, used only during the winter months. In summer, when the capital shifted from Delhi to Simla, Alipur House, like most buildings of Delhi, lay deserted and unused for six months at a stretch. It had anyway been built in 1917–18 as a temporary structure, to house the Commander-in-Chief's office till such time that a permanent abode could be made for it around Raisina Hill, the site of the new capital that the Government was contemplating. The foundations of the building were therefore not very deep. The roofs were *kutcha* (non-masonry), the walls were of bricks and clay, not mortar, and the verandahs, both front and back, were covered with *khappar* (clay tiles). Built during the First World War, when the construction rates were exceptionally high, its construction appears to be a rushed affair.

The exodus of the Commander-in-Chief and his staff from Alipur House to Raisina Hill began in 1926. The Indraprastha College management began its efforts to acquire the building, promising to lay here the foundation of a 'First Class' college for women in Delhi that would be open for all communities.

An unflagging correspondence ensued between Leonara G'meiner and the Chief Commissioner of Delhi. The latter had possibly entertained the idea of selling Alipur House to Indraprastha College. In 1925 itself, the Chief Commissioner had ascertained the value of the building, including the electric installations and other special services, at Rs 1,30,000. The college authorities had hesitated at the cost. They argued that the sum of Rs 1,30,000 for the building was the capital cost mentioned in the PWD books. Moreover, they reiterated that the building was constructed in 1917, when the rates were high owing to the war. Therefore, they insisted that the valuation of the building should be at current rates and reasonable depreciation should be allowed for the period from 1917 until the college was given possession of it. Secondly, regarding the payment of the purchase money, the college demanded that they should be allowed to make payments in installments of not more than Rs 5000 annually. This amount, the college management argued, was the maximum that they could raise and that too with great difficulty, particularly since the condition of trade in Delhi was exceedingly depressed. This indicates that the business community of Delhi was an important source of funds for the college.

However, even while the correspondence for the fixation of the value of the building and the purchase money was continuing, the Government expressed its inability to part with Alipur House as long as it was required for government purposes. It was almost certain that the house would be needed during the winter months of 1926–27 and may be even beyond. Meanwhile the New Capital Committee insisted that whenever Alipur House was put up for sale, it would be disposed off to the best advantage of the state. The hurdles to the acquisition of Alipur House multiplied but the college management was set on the house and kept up their demand of its first refusal whenever it was vacated.

It was apparent by 1927 that the British Government was impressed by the efforts of Indraprastha College to promote women's education. It also recognized the college's need for a larger accommodation. Consequently, in December 1927, the Government agreed to give the first refusal of Alipur House property to Indraprastha College but on certain terms and conditions: the land occupied by Alipur House would be given on perpetual lease; the period of first assessment of rent would be 31 March, 1950; the rest of the land would be leased as a playground on a ten-year lease without any option of renewal at Rs 25 per acre, and the building would be sold for Rs 1,25,000 payable in five installments of Rs 25,000. The Government offer came as a pleasant surprise to the college management committee. They were even more bewildered when the Government decided to make yet another concession. To help the college in meeting a portion of the cost of Alipur House, the Government proposed a grant of Rs 60,000 from the Central Revenue. Meanwhile, the college management sought financial support from the public to meet the cost of the building, the alterations and renovations it would require, and payment of the annual lease rent. Collections for two funds—Alipur House Building Fund and Alipur House Land Lease Endowment Fund—were initiated.

The government grant and assurances notwithstanding, the acquisition of Alipur House still seemed distant. By 1930, despite its promises, the Government appeared hesitant to dispense with Alipur House, at least for some years to come. Justifying its stand, the Government argued that the release of Alipur House was bound up with the future policy of construction of additional official residential accommodation in New Delhi. Significantly, even while the Government continued to ask for extended time to decide the fate of Alipur House and Indraprastha College, the All India Women's Education League under the guidance of Lady Irwin collected a large sum of money for a women teachers' training college to be established in Delhi. These efforts marked the beginnings of Lady Irwin College for Women for the study of Home Science, established in 1932. Appreciating the efforts of Lady Irwin, the authorities of Indraprastha

College urged that for a training college to flourish, it was absolutely necessary to have a degree college as a feeder. They emphasized that Indraprastha College was the only intermediate college for girls that could expand into a degree college as soon as the Government released Alipur House. The college committee asserted that over 600 girls, representing different communities and from almost all the provinces of India, had been educated by Indraprastha College. In such circumstances, the college committee argued that the prompt response of the Government regarding Alipur House would not only be deeply appreciated by the parents of the students but all such individuals who were linked with matters of education and the social upliftment of women of India.

However, the college was not given the possession of Alipur House even after the Commander-in-chief and his staff had shifted to New Delhi, as the PWD continued to use the building for other purposes. The college authorities filed an application in 1930 for Flagstaff House, then unoccupied. The college demanded the use of this House free of rent until the Government was in a position to give over the possession of Alipur House. But even as the college waited for the release of Alipur House, the Government rejected the application for Flagstaff House.

The government plans were soon revealed in a newspaper report. It was reported that with the onset of the winter of 1938, a number of government offices, including Military Accounts Office and Anti-Malaria Research Office, would transfer their headquarters to Delhi. And, since the Government faced dearth of accommodation in New Delhi, it would be necessary to utilize all government buildings in Old Delhi such as Flagstaff House that was so far being used by the Railway Conference Association and Alipur House, used till now for official residential purposes.[31] Also, Flagstaff House was reserved for Lady Irwin College (although the authorities of that college subsequently decided to remain in New Delhi).

STEPS INTO ALIPUR HOUSE

By 1937, Alipur House seemed a distant dream. The college's cherished desire to acquire Alipur House is evident in a letter Leonara G'meiner wrote to Lala Jagdish Prasad from Australia after her retirement: 'How often during the summer months, when the deserted Alipur House was tended only by a caretaker, accompanied by eager expectant

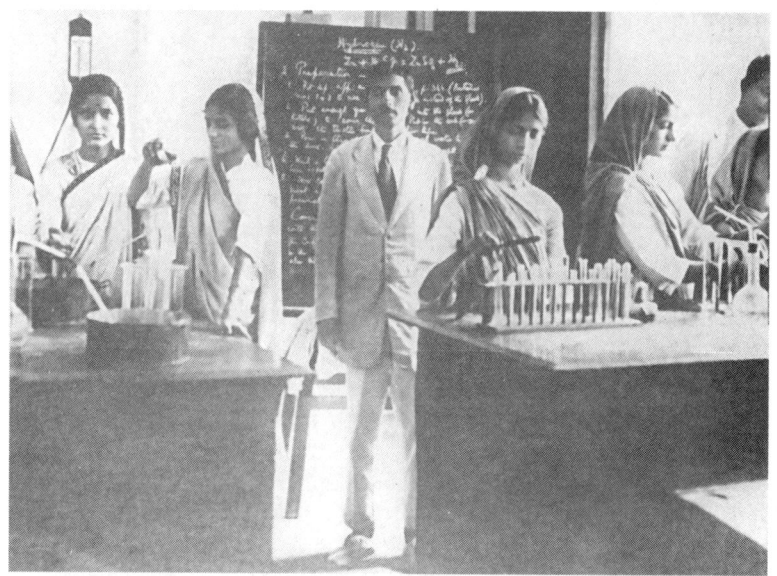

Indraprastha students at work in the science laboratory, May 1929.

Leonara G'meiner, the first Principal of Indraprastha School as well as of the College, with Lala Jugal Kishore, a founder member, outside Indraprastha School, where the college made its beginning in 1924.

Inauguration of Indraprastha College in Alipur House on 7 February, 1939 by Vicerine Lady Linlithgow. With her is Kalavati Gupta (in sari), the then Principal.

Faculty, February 1939
Standing: Mr G. Goswami, Pt T.N. Zutshi, Pt Ram Deva, Miss C.K. Kausukutty, Miss P. Sen Gupta
Sitting: Miss R. Sarkar, Miss B. Das Gupta, Miss J.K. Zutshi, Mrs B.P. Pillai

Sari-clad young Indraprastha students in a cooking class in 1929

Indraprastha students in 1939, rehearsing for a cultural programme on the back lawns of Alipur House. The mound (right, background) has been, since then, serving as an open-air theatre. Also seen (left, background) is the basketball court.

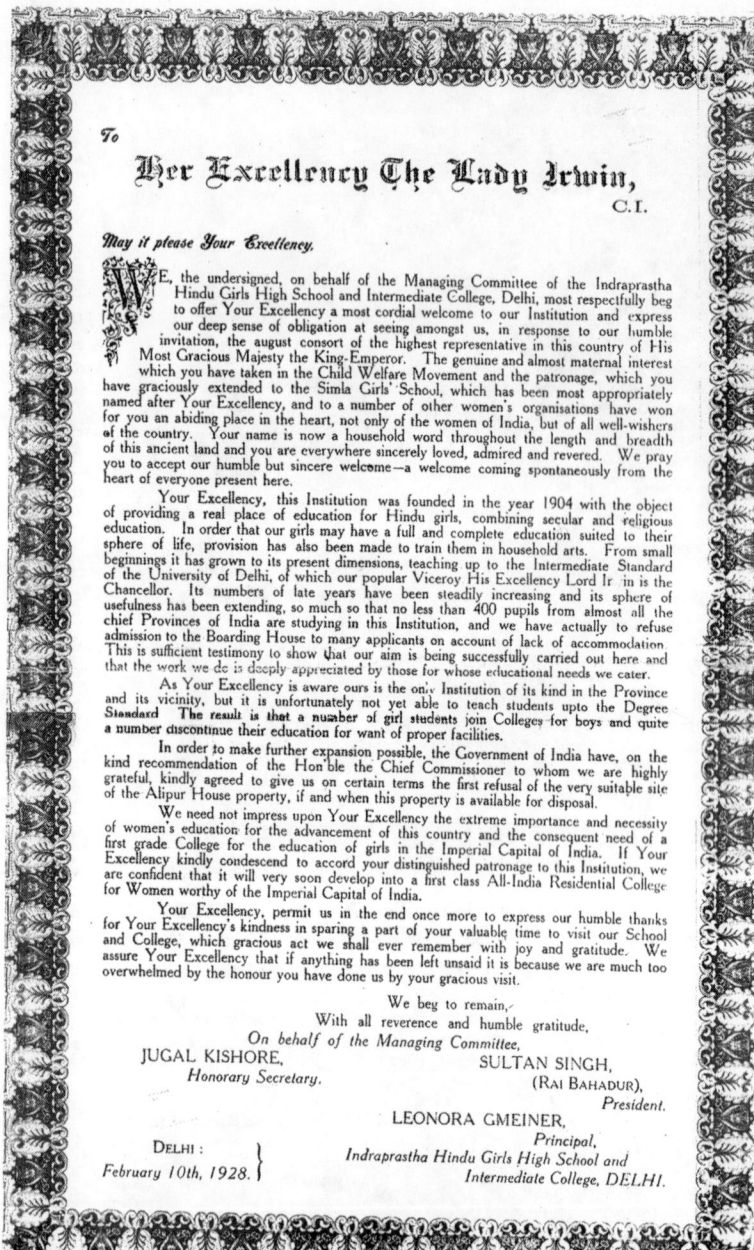

To

Her Excellency The Lady Irwin,
C.I.

May it please Your Excellency,

WE, the undersigned, on behalf of the Managing Committee of the Indraprastha Hindu Girls High School and Intermediate College, Delhi, most respectfully beg to offer Your Excellency a most cordial welcome to our Institution and express our deep sense of obligation at seeing amongst us, in response to our humble invitation, the august consort of the highest representative in this country of His Most Gracious Majesty the King-Emperor. The genuine and almost maternal interest which you have taken in the Child Welfare Movement and the patronage, which you have graciously extended to the Simla Girls' School, which has been most appropriately named after Your Excellency, and to a number of other women's organisations have won for you an abiding place in the heart, not only of the women of India, but of all well-wishers of the country. Your name is now a household word throughout the length and breadth of this ancient land and you are everywhere sincerely loved, admired and revered. We pray you to accept our humble but sincere welcome—a welcome coming spontaneously from the heart of everyone present here.

Your Excellency, this Institution was founded in the year 1904 with the object of providing a real place of education for Hindu girls, combining secular and religious education. In order that our girls may have a full and complete education suited to their sphere of life, provision has also been made to train them in household arts. From small beginnings it has grown to its present dimensions, teaching up to the Intermediate Standard of the University of Delhi, of which our popular Viceroy His Excellency Lord Ir in is the Chancellor. Its numbers of late years have been steadily increasing and its sphere of usefulness has been extending, so much so that no less than 400 pupils from almost all the chief Provinces of India are studying in this Institution, and we have actually to refuse admission to the Boarding House to many applicants on account of lack of accommodation. This is sufficient testimony to show that our aim is being successfully carried out here and that the work we do is deeply appreciated by those for whose educational needs we cater.

As Your Excellency is aware ours is the only Institution of its kind in the Province and its vicinity, but it is unfortunately not yet able to teach students upto the Degree Standard. The result is that a number of girl students join Colleges for boys and quite a number discontinue their education for want of proper facilities.

In order to make further expansion possible, the Government of India have, on the kind recommendation of the Hon'ble the Chief Commissioner to whom we are highly grateful, kindly agreed to give us on certain terms the first refusal of the very suitable site of the Alipur House property, if and when this property is available for disposal.

We need not impress upon Your Excellency the extreme importance and necessity of women's education for the advancement of this country and the consequent need of a first grade College for the education of girls in the Imperial Capital of India. If Your Excellency kindly condescend to accord your distinguished patronage to this Institution, we are confident that it will very soon develop into a first class All-India Residential College for Women worthy of the Imperial Capital of India.

Your Excellency, permit us in the end once more to express our humble thanks for Your Excellency's kindness in sparing a part of your valuable time to visit our School and College, which gracious act we shall ever remember with joy and gratitude. We assure Your Excellency that if anything has been left unsaid it is because we are much too overwhelmed by the honour you have done us by your gracious visit.

We beg to remain,

With all reverence and humble gratitude,

On behalf of the Managing Committee,

JUGAL KISHORE,
Honorary Secretary.

SULTAN SINGH,
(RAI BAHADUR),
President.

LEONORA GMEINER,
Principal,
Indraprastha Hindu Girls High School and
Intermediate College, DELHI.

DELHI :
February 10th, 1928.

Scroll presented to Vicerine Lady Irwin on her visit to Indraprastha School and College on 10 February 1928 little would-be college students, we roamed over the grounds, mentally marking out our tennis courts, basket ball ground and other sites for field sports; then laughingly the girls claimed their own quarters in the building and imagined erection of class rooms and 'Oh! a large hall for lectures, public gatherings and entertainment etc.'[32]

The Principal at that time, Kalavati Gupta, kept up efforts to acquire Alipur House, corresponding with and sending invitations to numerous official dignitaries to visit the college. One of those who visited was Lady Linlithgow, the Vicerine of India, in February 1937. She expressed her support of the college's demand for Alipur House, bolstering the college management's hopes. In 1937, Kalavati Gupta got wind of the fact that the Government had decided to release Alipur House for sale. She at once contacted Lady Linlithgow, who was on a furlough in England. Gupta was convinced that the Vicerine could ensure for the college the first refusal of Alipur House, something which had been promised by the Government all along, from as early as 1925. The Vicerine immediately cabled New Delhi and succeeded in securing Alipur House for Indraprastha College. It was given possession of Alipur House on 9 August 1938. To meet the cost of the building, the college made a contribution of Rs two lakhs from its Permanent Endowment Fund that was further supplemented by a government grant of Rs 60,000. The struggle for a spacious accommodation had lasted almost 13 years. The new premises were put to wider use from 6 October, 1938 although Lady Linlithgow formally inaugurated it on 7 February, 1939. The college is still located in this building and its beautiful grounds, and to this day has managed to preserve the sylvan surroundings and the charm of the bygone days.

The enthusiasm of the students knew no bounds at the possession of Alipur House. Sarla Sharma recalls that when the building was acquired, it was in the form of army barracks, surrounded by unkept grounds full of nettles. The girls, who felt a sense of pride at the triumph of the college after a long struggle, decided to clear the place. Within no time the students were mobilized and they volunteered to reach the college fifteen minutes before the classes began every morning, to pick the nettles. In a few days the whole place was cleared.[33] This strengthened the tradition of *shramdan* or selfless service that the students of this college often performed on several occasions.

Inspired by the acquisition of Alipur House, the college authorities initiated plans of strengthening the teaching staff and providing various amenities to the college. From a preliminary survey of the Alipur estate, it was felt necessary to provide the following immediately— a block for science lecture rooms and laboratories, residential quarters for teaching staff and hostels for students, a spacious hall, playground pavilion, swimming pool and fountains, a clock tower, and a small hospital. These targets appeared difficult to achieve in view of the perennial scarcity of funds. The college evolved a system for its maintenance: through the grants-in-aid from provincial revenues and municipal funds, donations and subscriptions from the public, interest on the college's Permanent Endowment fund, or rent from a few college properties. The sources of income on the surface seemed many but their returns to the college were meagre since they were utilized for the maintenance of not only the college but also Indraprastha School. However, the efforts of the college authorities were ably supported by the students who organized public plays, music concerts and fetes to raise money to facilitate the further expansion of the college.

As Indraprastha College settled into Alipur House, the college authorities set out to widen the horizon of its students. One of the processes was the development of sports facilities for its students. Immediately on shifting to Alipur House, the governing body of the college began the task of fulfilling the government order regarding the use of the six acres of land at the back of the college. At the time of the sale of Alipur House, the Government had ordained that this land should be developed as a play-field within three years of the grant. The college moved ahead to introduce and strengthen team games like netball, basketball, hockey, and volleyball. By 1942, two tennis courts were provided for, although there were no facilities for athletics till 1940. The college authorities sent some students to the National Stadium (in a college bus escorted by a woman chaperon) to learn the techniques of athletics. These endeavours appeared positive when one of its students, Savitri Dang, brought glory to the college between 1939 and 1941 in the field of athletics. She stood first not only in the intra-college athletics meet but also in the inter-college women's athletics meet in Delhi.[34] Savitri Dang made the college proud by becoming the first woman Delhi State champion in athletics.

Science Classes: An Unfulfilled Dream

Even though the science stream could not be ultimately introduced in the college, the earnest efforts of the college authorities to implement this dream cannot be doubted. In April 1937, the Governing Body and the Board of Trustees decided to start science classes to meet the pressing demand of the public. They filed applications for the recognition of science classes by Delhi University and also for securing a special grant from the Government to facilitate the opening of these classes. The college management stressed the urgency of opening a new department of science by pointing out the fact that Lady Hardinge Medical College had decided to discontinue its pre-medical classes. In the absence of these classes since May 1937, Indraprastha College had received several applications from women students for admission to intermediate science classes.

The college's desire to introduce science classes was also a response to the difficulties faced by the students—both men and women—of Delhi in professional education, an issue that was widely discussed during that period, occupying large spaces in most of the newspapers. While Delhi offered sufficient facilities for ordinary collegiate education, there were no provisions in the city for professional courses like medicine, engineering, or teaching. The students keen on pursuing these courses had to join Universities in other provinces. But, even in these Universities, the pressure of their own state's students had increased, rendering the chances of admission difficult for the students of Delhi. With the grant of Provincial Autonomy by the Government of India in 1937, there was an added apprehension that the provinces might become parochial and close their doors to the students from the other provinces. In such an event, it was necessary to seek the help of the Government for opening professional colleges in Delhi. It was felt that there was a good case for opening a medical college for men in Delhi because apart from the fact that Delhi offered good scope for hospital training of all kinds, such a college would serve not only the Delhi province but also the adjoining states that could be persuaded to provide some financial help in the foundation of a medical college. Moreover, considering the rising demand for education in Delhi, the case for a training college for teachers was equally strong. It was observed that Delhi could not always be dependent on Lahore and Lucknow for its teachers. Till professional training and professional courses were introduced in Delhi, arrangements should be made with the adjoining state Universities for reservation of seats for students from Delhi, otherwise students eager on securing professional education may find themselves stranded.[35]

The issue of women students was discussed more specifically, especially in the context of the decision of Lady Hardinge Medical College to close intermediate science classes. This decision had adversely affected girls, particularly from Delhi, who were keen on a science education. To ensure the careers of their daughters, the parents made fervent appeals to Indraprastha College to introduce science classes, something it had been contemplating for so many years. The fear was that if Indraprastha College made any further delay in introducing the science classes, the Delhi girls, who wished to study science, would have to depend on men's colleges which were already overcrowded or alternatively go to Lucknow, Lahore, or some other place. If the girls were compelled to resort to the latter, it would certainly be hard on them, considering the additional expenses and the problem of shifting from their homes. In such a situation, the desire of the girls for higher education could remain unfulfilled. To prevent such an eventuality, it was necessary to persuade the British Government into providing financial aid to Indraprastha College to facilitate the introduction of science classes. Hoping to exert pressure on the Government, a *Hindustan Times* report said: 'it would be a sad confession for the Imperial City if it cannot offer sufficient facilities for its girl students.'[36]

Responding to this news item of 31 May, 1937 in *The Hindustan Times*, the honorary secretary of the college, Lala Jagdish Prasad, expressed the college's desire to start science classes as early as possible. But, since the hurdles were many, time was required and science classes, at the earliest, could be introduced only by May 1938.[37] By February 1939, the governing body of the college had become more cautious in its statements on introducing science classes. It declared that before any decision on the introduction of science classes could be taken, the view of the Education Department in the Government of India would have to be ascertained on the possibility and the extent of financial assistance—both capital as well as recurring grants-in-aid from the Government. The introduction of science classes would depend on government aid and public donations. But, despite their efforts, the college authorities could not raise sufficient funds nor receive government support to introduce science classes.

MATTERS RELATING TO TEACHERS

In the late 1930s the college embarked on the process of formalization and organization of the work and salary of the teachers as per the University and government regulations. It is worth mentioning here that though the college authorities had never succumbed to government pressure to intervene in or ban anti-government student activities and their participation in the freedom struggle, yet in the appointment of teachers, they were discreet and cautious. Prior to confirming the appointment of any lecturer, the college management asked the prospective lecturers to give a written assurance to the effect that they would not involve themselves in politics and political propaganda or abet any disruptive political activity. In an atmosphere charged with challenges to the authority of the British Government, such declarations of abstinence from politics were perhaps deemed necessary to convince the Government that the college remained aloof and indifferent to national politics and thus ensure government grants-in-aid to the college.

These years were also marked by power struggles and personality clashes between the trustees and the governing body of the college. Throughout 1939, they remained in a state of conflict over the appointment of teachers and the Principal of the college. Although the college functioned under the University statute, the new statute of 1939 gave the governing body complete control over the affairs of the college. This caused a controversy between the Board of Trustees and the governing body, particularly over the appointment of the Principal. The issue was—who should make the appointment— the Board of Trustees or the governing body? This debate was further ignited by the example of St. Stephen's College, the Principal of which was appointed not by the governing body but by the Supreme Council. To resolve the issue before it became even more complex, most of the trustees agreed that the appointment of the teaching staff, including the Principal, should be a matter under the jurisdiction of the governing body.

The conflict between the trustees and the governing body erupted once again in June 1939 over the appointment of a qualified auditor to audit the accounts of the college. The secretary of the Board of Trustees insisted that it was within their jurisdiction to appoint the auditor. The members of the governing body, on the other hand, argued that since they were responsible for the planning and approval of the annual accounts of the college, the privilege to appoint the auditor belonged to them. The matter could be resolved only in October 1939 when the trustees and the governing body agreed to act in tandem and in consultation with each other regarding the appointment of the auditor.

With the expansion of the college, there was a need to fill up the vacancies in teaching posts. By June 1939, the college could identify the immediate necessity of at least two teachers qualified to teach the following combination of subjects—English; English and Philosophy; English and Economics; Economics and Philosophy. But, despite the need for teachers, the appointment of teaching staff for English, Philosophy, and Economics was postponed since the college could not fulfil at least one of the terms insisted upon by the University—it could not ascertain the extent and the nature of work done by the existing teachers. In principle, the governing body of the college understood the necessity of defining hours of work but it believed that it was premature to legislate exact maximum hours of teaching unless the cooperative system of teaching was introduced by the University. The governing body opposed the University on yet another matter viz the University's letter of December 1938 regarding the number of recognized teachers in any college of Delhi University. It expressed its strong reservations against the fixing of a student–teacher ratio, particularly at a time when women's education was in the process of its development. The governing body reiterated that since the resources and the financial status of the different colleges of Delhi University were at variance with each other, the management of each college should be given a greater freedom in fixing the number of recognized teachers. For Indraprastha College, the governing body felt that 1:30 (1 teacher for 30 students) would be a satisfactory ratio. While the debate on the extent and hours of work of the teachers continued, R.W. Ghate and Nirmala Sherjung were appointed in October 1939 by Indraprastha College as lecturers in the departments of Economics and Philosophy respectively. Both of them were also asked to teach English. Teaching of English, till the late 1930s required a mere knowledge of the English language; no additional qualifications or specialization were insisted upon. However, changes set in from the late 1930s and early 1940s, when the students demanded the teaching of English as a separate subject. Responding to the demand, a member of the governing body, Rai Bahadur Ram Kishore, suggested the idea of creating a department of English in the college, which soon became a reality in the 1940s.

In this process of reorganization of the college, hours and nature of work of the teachers was not the only issue. The governing body of the college also contemplated fixing grades of salaries for its teachers. But before they could take a decision, the University of Delhi passed an ordinance in 1938 for uniform salaries for all the teachers of Delhi University. The teachers of Indraprastha College, justifiably, demanded the revision of their salaries as per the University ordinance. The governing body withheld the demand of the teachers until the University ordinance actually became effective. It argued that in principle it approved the salaries prescribed by the University. But in 1939, when the college faced a variety of financial obligations, it could not adopt an upper limit of salaries, as suggested by the University. In defence of its argument, the governing body reiterated that in 1937–38 the college had purchased Alipur House and subsequently the alterations and additions to the building had entailed a substantial expenditure. The governing body further argued that if despite the limited financial resources of the college, the University insisted on fixing minimum salary by an ordinance, it would have to give all the colleges, not only Indraprastha College, sufficient time to implement the ordinance. The governing body added yet another proviso to its suggestion, without however substantiating it—the teachers teaching modern Indian languages and translations should be paid lower salaries.

It is evident from these arguments that the governing body of Indraprastha College was persistently engaged in consolidating its power vis-á-vis the University in the latter half of the 1930s. This attitude was most apparent over the issue of grades of salary of teachers and the payment of increments to them. The reaction of the college management in March 1939 to the circular from the University on the implementation of conditions of service of teachers is interesting. It argued that the question of increment to the teachers was a matter of contract between the employer and the employee and that the University could interfere only on issues like the maintenance of proper standard in the college.

Notwithstanding the resistance of the governing body of the college, the late 1930s and especially the year 1939 were focused on the formalization and implementation of the University and government regulations in Delhi University. The endeavour was to achieve uniformity in all colleges of Delhi University. As the power and the control of the University over the colleges increased, the governing bodies of all the colleges in Delhi University became even more resistant and assertive.

WIDENING HORIZONS

The disputes over the grades of salaries of teachers had little impact on the commitment of the teachers in Indraprastha College. Together with the students, they continued to widen the college's horizon in academic and extra-curricular activities.

Till 1939 there was no students' union. But there were student societies representing different interests, harnessing literary talents, and developing the aptitude of the students for social service and sports. Most of the student societies evolved and developed under the patronage of Janak Kumari Zutshi, a lecturer in the department of English in the 1930s. To stimulate literary interest amongst the students, Zutshi started 'The Torch Bearer Society' in 1937. The significant feature of the society was an annual hand-written magazine called *The Torch Bearer*, which contained stories and poems by the students, both in English and Hindi, and also sketches and paintings. The aim of the magazine, as the then editor reported, was to improve the standard of English amongst the students. It was also 'to give a chance to the girls to develop their tastes and hobbies' and encourage them as 'budding poetesses, artists, story-writers and so forth otherwise their talents could remain hidden for lack of opportunity.'[38] An essay in the first number of *The Torch Bearer*, 'Female Education in India', can be taken as representative of the views of educated women of the 1930s. A critique on contemporary female education, it posits that the importance of education lay only in enhancing the value of the girls in the marriage market: 'Very few of these (educated girls) have any intentions of taking up any profession afterwards. Most of them join college to pass their time and some others just to increase their value in the marriage market'. The writer sarcastically suggests that instead of opening new colleges for girls, 'a school of domestic science for girls' should be established. In such schools, 'time and labour will not be wasted but such education will enable them to live their life as wife and mother in a cleverer, better and happier way.'[39]

The students were encouraged to publish the first issue of the college magazine, *Pradeep*, in 1939. Since then, the college magazine has become the annual feature of the college. The name of the magazine, over the years, has changed from *Pradeep* to *Silhouette* to *Aaroh*. Also, the focus of the articles in the magazine then and now are remarkably different. The editorials and articles of the students of those days were thought-provoking, reflecting social and political concerns. It was apparent that the students, in the midst of the national movement, Second World War, and various other developments and conflicts at the national and international level, were influenced by and engaged with them. The current *Aaroh* represents a responsible student no doubt, but it also exhibits an attitude born and bred in a free but complex India—a mix of fun, restlessness, and cynicism.

In 1939, the idea of a students' union was also concretized. To govern themselves and regulate their activities, the Students' Union gave themselves a constitution, the significant feature of which was that only the first-and the third-year students were entitled to be office-bearers. Recognizing the significance of the institution to which they belonged, the students devised a badge and a motto of the college. The Students' Union of 1939 emphasized the need for organizing an old students' association, to revive the memories of the past and relive the experiences of some of the first students of this pioneering school and college.

To the already existing Literary Society, Debating Society and the Games Committee were added the Entertainment Committee, Social Service League, and the Hindustani Association. The purpose of the Hindustani Association was to encourage and spread the learning of Hindi and Urdu among the students so as to develop a language that could foster common bonds. The Hindustani Association was an attempt at teaching Hindi to those who knew Urdu and vice versa. To ensure that the students took their task seriously, examinations were held for the language concerned and as an incentive, certificates were distributed to the successful candidates. The Social Service League was a move to inculcate social awareness and a sense of national harmony and responsibility amongst the students. The League organized students' visits to villages in the vicinity of the college to impart lessons in health and hygiene and to emphasize the importance of literacy. In their visits to the neighbouring villages and *bastis*, the students cut across caste lines, undaunted by the caste-oriented conservatism of their families.

As one browses through the *Pradeep* of 1939, the thoughts, concerns, and personalities of the students emerge clearly. We are transported to the upheaval of those days. The editorial appropriately called 'Inqlab', expressed the girls' desire for freedom, their opinion on world politics and British imperialism, and their resentment of India being compelled into joining the Second World War. The disappointment and the anger of the young at the mishandling of world politics by the imperialist powers was further aroused by Jawaharlal Nehru's presidential address to the Lucknow Congress in 1936 where he stated the Congress's opposition to India's participation in a war between the imperialist powers and offered India's co-operation to the progressive forces of the world, to those that stood for freedom and the breaking of political and social bondage. Inspired by national leaders, the students of Indraprastha College imbibed the spirit of *Inqlab Zindabad.* And, as India became increasingly involved in the Second World War, the students of the college, mobilized themselves to oppose and challenge British imperialism.

NOTES AND REFERENCES

1. The observations on the responses and reactions of the students of Indraprastha College are based on an interview with Sarla Sharma, a student of the college in the years 1936–40.

2. Bimla Luthra, 'Nehru and the Place of Women in Indian Society' in B.R. Nanda (ed.), *Indian Women: From Purdah to Modernity*, Vikas Publishing House, New Delhi, 1996, p. 2.

3. Kumari Jayawardene, 'Women, Social Reform and Nationalism in India' in Kumari Jayawardene, *Feminism and Nationalism in the Third World*, p. 99.

4. Jawaharlal Nehru, *The Discovery of India*, New Delhi, 1964, pp. 41–2.

5. Sunaina Sharma and Madhu Kishwar, 'Toofani Satyawati: An Unsung Hero of Freedom Struggle' in *Manushi*, No. 107, July–August 1998, p. 25.

6. Aparna Basu, 'The Role of Women in the Indian Struggle for Freedom' in B.R. Nanda (ed.), *Indian Women: From Purdah to Modernity*, p. 27.

7. Interview with Sarla Sharma.

8. F.F. Monk, *A History of St. Stephens College, Delhi*, pp. 233–4.

9. Interview with Sarla Sharma.

10. Aparna Basu, 'The Role of Women in the Indian Struggle For Freedom', pp. 27–9.

11. Narayani Gupta, *Delhi Between Two Empires, 1803–1931*, Oxford University Press, New Delhi, 1981, p. 221.

12. S. Ram Sharma, *Women and Education*, Vol. III of *Women's Education and National Awakening*, Discovery Publications, 1995, p. 162.

13. 'A Delhi Appeal' by Lala Jugal Kishore, Honorary Secretary of the Governing Body of Indraprastha Girls' College, *The Leader*, 10 September, 1932.

14. Interview with Monta Bose, a student of the college from 1931 to 1933. She later joined the college as a lecturer in the Department of Economics and continued to serve here till her retirement in December 1981.

15. 'Delhi Girls' Education: Record of Progress of Indraprastha Girls' School', *The National Call*, 16 April, 1934.

16. Interview with Sarla Sharma.

17. Correspondence with Shanti Nigam, a student of Indraprastha School from 1929 and then of Indraprastha College from 1934 to 1938.

18. Interview with Prem Mukhi Saxena, a student of the college in 1935–39. She joined the college as a lecturer in the Department of History in 1942 and worked there till her retirement in 1986.

19. Sarla Sharma, 'Rashtriya Andolan Mein Indraprastha', in *The Golden Oriole, 1924–74* (a special issue of the college magazine to celebrate the Golden Jubilee of the college). Shanti Nigam expressed similar sentiments in her correspondence with us.

20. Interview with Sarla Sharma.

21. Sarla Sharma, 'Sangeet Roopak, 1929-47' (unpublished).

22. Convocation Address at the University of Delhi by the Vice-Chancellor, Professor M. Abdur Rahman, 1931.

23. 'Indraprastha College Facing Crisis: Financial Stringency: Negotiations Proceeding With Govt. of India', *The Hindustan Times*, 16 May, 1933.

24. 'Indraprastha Girls' College', *The Hindustan Times*, 23 November, 1934.

25. Letter to the Editor by Kalavati Gupta, the Principal, and Lala Jugal Kishore, Honorary Secretary of the College Management, entitled 'Indraprastha Girls' College: Remarkable Progress: No Demand for Overhaul of Policy', *The Hindustan Times*, 28 November, 1934.

26. 'Viceroy's Sympathy with Moslems', *The Statesman*, 29 October, 1936.

27. Ibid.

28. Ibid.

29. Ibid.

30. Letter from Leonara G'meiner to Lala Jugal Kishore, 16 April, 1935.

31. 'Government Buildings Causing Anxiety About Alipore House', *The Hindustan Times*, 9 June, 1937.

32. Letter from Leonara G'meiner to Lala Jagdish Prasad.

33. Sarla Sharma, 'Rashtriya Andolan Mein Indraprastha'.

34. At that time, there were two other women's colleges—Lady Irwin College and Lady Hardinge Medical College.

35. 'Professional Education: Difficulties of Delhi Students', *The Hindustan Times*, 31 May, 1937.

36. Ibid.

37. Letter to the Editor entitled 'Indraprastha Girls' College To Start Science Classes', *The Hindustan Times*, 1 June, 1937.

38. *The Torch Bearer* (hand-written college magazine), May 1937.

39. Uma Joshi, 'Female Education in India' in *The Torch Bearer*, May 1937.

4

From *Purdah* to Politics:
Defying *Zalim Sarkar,* 1940–47

The years 1940–47 marked the zenith of India's freedom struggle. Imbibing the national fervour, women in all parts of India were in the forefront of national protests and the freedom movement, joining processions and demonstrations addressed by the national leaders. In Delhi, which by 1940 had become an epicentre of politics, women participated in protest marches and rallies in large numbers. From amongst these, a significant section came from Indraprastha College. Dressed in hand-woven (sometimes by the students themselves) rough, white *khadi saris,* they joined the anti-government processions and occasionally even led them, singing '*Nahi Rakhni, Nahi Rakhni, Zalim Sarkar, Nahi Rakhni...*' Whenever they heard of meetings being addressed by leaders such as Gandhi and Nehru in the vicinity of the college, they rushed to listen to them. Neither college regulations nor the formality of seeking the Principal's permission made them hesitate in such plans.[1] The behaviour of these students exemplify the power, independence, and courage of women of those days.

A CONSOLIDATED STUDENTS' MOVEMENT

To defy the British Raj and engage with the national movement in a consolidated way, several students joined the All India Students' Federation (AISF) formed in 1936. The purpose of the AISF was to create social awareness in the Indian student community. The AISF represented all shades of ideologies—Congress, Communist, Socialist—and yet stood together as a united body of students. However, the influence of communism began to be increasingly felt in the organization. Many students of Indraprastha College who were staunch Gandhians and devoted Congress workers came under its sway.[2] This trend was not peculiar to Indraprastha College; it was widely noticed amongst women students in different parts of India. At this time, the AISF set up a Girls Students Committee to mobilize militant young women in different parts of the country. This effort received enthusiastic support from the provinces of Bengal, Bombay, and Punjab. In Delhi, the mobilization was not as strong though a number of students did join the committee.[3]

The girl students' movement organized by the AISF grew rapidly throughout India. By 1941 its membership had risen to 50,000, and it had become a source of inspiration for many young women. Several of them were so intensely involved in political activities that they even left their homes. Even the possibility of being arrested could not daunt their spirit.[4] This kind of enthusiasm was also evident amongst many students of Indraprastha College. When we spoke to Sarla Sharma, it seemed that the memory of her comrades and their activities was still fresh in her mind. She rattled off a number of names—Rashida, Fahmida, Vibha, Indra, Pran, Reva Roy, Usha Malik—who, along with her, were active AISF members and supported the communist ideology. Two of them—Zohra Ansari and Nafisa—Sarla Sharma mentioned as significant examples of committed communist activists.[5] To mobilize student support, Sarla Sharma said, AISF members moved around on bicycles, distributing communist party literature in every college. She narrated to us her encounter with Professor V.K.R.V. Rao of the Delhi School of Economics. It seems that when she gave him the party literature, he threw it on the ground, saying he did not agree with it. Undaunted by his tantrum and ignoring the fact that he was a professor of one of the eminent institutions of India, she accused him of being a fascist, asked him to pick up the literature from the ground, pay 4 annas (which was its cost), read it, and discuss it even if he did not agree with it. Sharma recounted with pride that Professor Rao did as she bade him. Her success, she claims, was not momentary. They became friends although they differed ideologically.[6]

1942: AGITATION, PARTICIPATION, EXPERIENCE

The failure of the Cripps Mission in 1942 embittered most Indians. There was now more determination to oust the British from power and compel them to accept the demand for India's independence. On 8 August 1942, the All India Congress Committee met in Bombay and passed the Quit India resolution calling for the withdrawal of the British from India. The Congress proclaimed the intensification of the non-violent mass struggle under the leadership of Gandhi and advised the people that until further orders from the Congress 'every man and woman ... must function for himself or herself within the four corners of the general instructions issued.'[7] The Quit India resolution directly addressed women 'as disciplined soldiers of Indian freedom' and encouraged them to join the movement.[8] Gandhi urged the people to take up in earnest non-violent techniques such as salt making, boycott of British courts and schools, picketing of foreign cloth and liquor shops, and non-payment of taxes. The British Government reacted sharply to this increasing challenge to its power. The Government arrested the Congress leaders on 9 August 1942 barely a day after the Quit India Movement was announced. Mass protests followed the arrest of the leaders. Unperturbed by government severity, the people continued their attack on all symbols of state authority.[9] Soon after his arrest, when Gandhi went on fast, the students and teachers of Delhi University led by V.K.R.V. Rao took out a procession to pray for his well being. For several days, the atmosphere was tense, classes were not held, and there was police action against those who had participated.[10] However, the determination of the people rendered the coercive actions of the police look ineffectual. The Quit India Movement became widespread in the cities as strikes, demonstrations, and clashes with the police occurred all over. Within no time, it moved to the countryside, where peasants rebelled against landowners and all representations of British authority. Women participated actively in strikes and demonstrations in the cities. Some of them helped in organizing peasant movements and when the Government used repressive measures against them, they went underground to continue their activities.[11] Aruna Asaf Ali was one of the important leaders of the 1942 movement. For four years, she remained underground, evading arrest. But she continued to arouse the people and mobilize them by publishing bulletins and the magazine called *Inquilab* that she edited with Ram Manohar Lohia.

Her power was so intense that the British Government was compelled to announce a reward of Rs 5000 for her arrest.[12]

Aruna Asaf Ali had a deep impact on several students of Indraprastha College as can be illustrated by the recollections of Rup Seth, a student of the college from 1940 to 1944. During the Quit India Movement, a group of girls from the college assisted Aruna Asaf Ali in pasting anti-British posters on the walls of the city of Delhi. They were, as was the norm in those days, arrested for their anti-government activities. However, no obstructionist tactics of the Government could challenge the spirit of these girls—as Rup Seth put it, the 'daredevils' of Indraprastha College hoisted the tricolour in the premises of the jail.[13] In fact, several students of the college who had participated in the Quit India Movement were jailed for two to three months or even more.[14] Vijaya Mehrotra and other students of the college who were jailed during the Quit India Movement found themselves rusticated from college, as per government orders, on their release from jail. They appealed to the vice chancellor, who considered their case sympathetically and ordered the repeal of their rustication from college.[15] The constant government coercion spurred the Indraprastha girls, like other Indians, to further action. To protest the arrest of the national leaders and, demand their release, 10,000 students marched in a procession led by Sarla Sharma. Although the students were non-violent throughout the procession, the police reacted by *lathi* charge and teargassing. None of these tactics deterred the students. They used self-defence methods to protect themselves and remained adamant in their struggle. Of her experiences of 1942, Sarla Sharma says: 'we then did not fear or avoid arrest. In fact, we volunteered to court arrest...in the perspective of 1942, our urge was to meet, express and publish our views.'[16] Other women leaders who inspired the students included Satyawati (granddaughter of the social reformer, Mahatma Munshi Ram, later known as Swami Shraddhanand) who actively participated in the Quit India Movement and exhorted the students to become the vanguards of the movement.[17]

The girls of the college debated whether to study for the examinations and degrees or plunge into the Quit India Movement. The girls rejected neither their studies nor the national call for fighting for independence. One incident in striking—when the AISF gave a call for anti-British protest, the girls of Indraprastha College jumped the walls of the college to join the boys of St. Stephen's and Hindu College, to participate in a the students' procession in support of the Quit India Movement.[18] Ajit Bhattacharya, a student of St. Stephen's then, recounts the episode: On 10 August 1942 a 'vociferous gathering of Hinduites and ladies from Indraprastha College collected outside the gates of St. Stephen's and urged Stephanians to join them in a procession to support the Congress leaders who had been jailed the previous day. About half the college made its way out through the back gate [of St. Stephen's] and across the university grounds to join the demonstrators. The crowd marched down Alipur Road, passing en route IP college whose authorities had shut the gates to prevent the remaining girls from joining in. They resourcefully jumped down the walls assisted by willing Stephanian hands and the procession continued down Chandni Chowk, shouting slogans led by an enthusiastic and loud-voiced fresher named Akhilesh Mittal.'[19] That the involvement of the students of Indraprastha College in the freedom struggle was complete is evident from the fact that the students' union organized virtually no academic or entertainment programmes in 1942. The union remained solely engaged in planning and hosting general strikes and protests, and demanding the release of the national leaders—a recurring pattern all over the nation.

The students, whole-hearted involvement in the freedom movement can be gauged from an event of 1942. A team from Indraprastha College was sent to participate in the Olympics of 1942.[20] It emerged as the runners-up in the netball competition. But the excitement of being runners-up in the Olympics soon waned when the students heard of the Quit India Movement and the arrest of the national leaders on 9 August 1942. At the function organized to celebrate the team's success the students shouted anti-British slogans and protested against the arrest of the national leaders. Vicerine Lady Linlithgow too was present there. Offended by the behaviour of the students, she complained to the governing body of the college. The members of the governing body, felt a sense of obligation towards her because of her efforts at securing Alipur House for the college, and had no option but to apologize to her and instruct the principal to take disciplinary action against these students. The students were warned of severe consequences in case of any such activity in future.

As an active participant in the Quit India Movement, Indraprastha College was quickly identified by the British Government as one of the centres of political activity and trouble, and pressure tactics were applied on the college. The Superintendent of Education complained to the governing body about the 'indifferent discipline' in the college, in an apparent reference to the agitationist activities of the students and arrest of some of them. On this pretext, he threatened to withhold the government grant to the college.[21] This was an oft-repeated ploy of the Government: it knew fully well how important government grants were for the survival of the colleges of Delhi University. With the knowledge of the indispensability of government grants hanging over their heads, the governing body of the college responded to the Superintendent of Education's letter by advising the Principal, Kalavati Gupta, to prepare an exhaustive report on the alleged acts of indiscipline of the students; the names of those who had participated in activities relating to the Quit India Movement were to be cited. The Principal sought to exonerate the students, saying their activities were impulsive, born of spontaneous urges. She refused to divulge the names of the students and thus none of them were victimized.[22] The Government threats could not prevent the Principal from supporting the national cause by providing tacit and discreet support to her students.

Their Principal's sympathetic attitude and silent consent further emboldened the students. They continued to participate in the political deliberations and strikes throughout 1942. The Government carried out a sustained pressure compaign on the institution. One of its tactics was to send officials from the Public Works Department on the pretext of inspecting the college building. The governing body apprehended it as a government move to deprive the college of its building as a punishment for the students' active participation in the national movement. Their fears were not unfounded. Colleges such as Ramjas were also sent government warnings for their students' involvement in the freedom struggle. As in the case of Indraprastha College, the Education Department had sent a letter to Ramjas College warning that unless discipline was restored and the students resumed attending classes, the recurring maintenance grants made from the Central Revenue Department would be cancelled for the financial year, that is, 1942–43.[23]

In September 1942, the Government cancelled the wheat permit of the hostels of three colleges of Delhi University viz. Indraprastha College, Hindu College, and Commercial College, without assigning any reasons for the order. What was surprising was the cancellation of the wheat permit of just these three hostels while there were more than a dozen hostels in the other colleges of Delhi University. The order caused much resentment. The newspapers termed it a political move, 'a sort of omnibus vendetta for any sins of omission or commission' which in the opinion of the controller of wheat, the students of these colleges may have committed individually or collectively. They criticized the order as 'inhuman and barbaric' and as a 'calculated meanness repugnant to the vital traditions of chivalry both of India and Great Britain.'[24] Their contention was that even if the students of these colleges and their hostels were engaged in political warfare against the Government, cutting off of food supplies could never be deemed a fair and legitimate weapon. The cut in the food supplies to these hostels, however, continued till 1945.

The immediate cause of the cancellation of the wheat permit for Indraprastha College seemed to be the fact that the girls of the college had participated in the '*rakhi* expedition', that is, they had sent *rakhis* to their Muslim brethren to emphasize Hindu-Muslim unity and communal harmony.[25] By 1942, the Government, had successfully created a wedge between the two communities. Therefore, this action of the students did not meet with its approval. Charging the students with fuelling political carnage, the Government punished them by depriving them of their food supplies.

The Government cuts and orders did not succeed in cowing down the students, as evident from what transpired at the annual function of the college in 1943. The rationing orders threatened to disrupt the tea party slated for the day and create an embarrassing situation. The Students' Union of the college responded in a mature way. They collected contributions from the students of the college, hosted the tea party, and thereby overcame a crisis that could have caused a loss of face to the college. A hypothetical conversation between a teacher and students of the college published in a newspaper illustrates the students' attitude:

Indraprastha College Teacher: Girls enumerate to me the many blessings of the British Raj
Students speaking all at once said: railways, telephones... whisky, beer... high-heeled shoes... airplanes... ICS
Teacher (reacting to the students' excitement) asked again: Any more?
One girl replied: The Wheat Controller[26]

Such anecdotes suggest that the rationing orders or the cut in the wheat supply to the hostels had not dampened the enthusiasm of the students. However, in the circumstances when Government pressures were becoming increasingly severe, the governing body of the College urged the Principal to restore discipline amongst the students. Failing to prevail upon the students to attend classes or control the student agitation, the Principal, as a last resort, wrote letters of complaint to the parents/guardians of the students in September 1942. The first letter of warning was sent on 3 September, 1942. The complaint was that since 10 August, 1942, in support of the Quit India Movement and to protest against the arrest of the national leaders, the students had cut classes even though they came to college. In other words, the college was open but the students observed *hartal*, organized meetings in the campus, made fiery speeches, and mobilized themselves for political activities. They could not be controlled by the Principal or by the teachers. Consequently, on most days since 10 August, 1942, they were sent back home after an hour or so. The Principal said that only if their daughters agreed to attend classes, would the college buses be sent to their homes to pick them up. The parents were asked to reply in the affirmative by 6 September, 1942. But the seemingly urgent appeal of the Principal failed to move either the parents or the students. There was no response to the Principal's letter. The Principal was compelled to write another, sterner, letter, on 7 September, 1942 in which she complained that the students were not only abstaining from classes but also using picketing and other coercive methods against such students who attended classes. She had refrained from any drastic step because of her faith in the good sense of the students but in the circumstances, when the Government was becoming increasingly repressive and arbitrary, it had become necessary for her to ensure uninterrupted work and discipline in the college. The parents were thus asked to advise their daughters to either attend classes or withdraw from the college. The Principal sought the cooperation of the parents of each girl in ensuring that their 'daughter comes to the college only for study and for nothing else'. She reiterated her commitment to avoid invoking the help of any 'outside body or to take any unpleasant step'.

The events of 1942 influenced the personalities of almost all the students of Indraprastha College. Recounting her experiences, Shanta Vashisht, a practising civil lawyer in Delhi who graduated in 1944, said that in 1942 when the atmosphere was surcharged with patriotism, the teachers and the students of the college worked in tandem, with the former inducing national fervour amongst the students. Such was the involvement of the students in the movement that when the political prisoners at Deoli camp went on hunger strike, the whole college also observed a one-day sympathetic hunger strike. It was probably for the first time that the hostel kitchen remained closed.[27] Another former student, Sucharita Sen Gupta, recalls the intense involvement of the girls in the 1942 movement—shouting slogans, organizing long meetings, singing patriotic songs, and missing no opportunity to defy the rules and regulations fixed by the British Government.[28] With the same enthusiasm, Protima Mukerji, another former IP-ite, writes that the Quit India Movement and the arrest of the national leaders had 'turned the students into miniature politicians orating on the college platform and passing resolutions in support of the movement'. From then, she says, had begun the tradition of singing patriotic songs during morning prayers in the college.[29]

Nilima Chakravarty and Nirmala Prakash, two former students as well as former teachers of the college, nostalgically remember the student agitation of the 'stormy August days of 1942' and the student resistance to the appeals of the then Principal, K. Ranga Rao, to stay away from political strikes and demonstrations.[30] Nirmala Prakash recalls that despite the orders of Ranga Rao, she mobilized the students of the college and lectured to them for hours in the college lawns, urging them to join the national strikes, demonstrations, and processions against the Government. Several of them, she writes, also attended mass rallies and moved from street to street, shouting slogans and courting arrest. In the same spirit and enthusiasm, the students initiated the idea of a *charkha* association in the college. The Principal discouraged the proposal for fear that if she permitted any activity associated with the national movement, it might incite the Government to impose prohibitory orders on the college and withdraw its grant.[31] The apprehensions of the Principal, however, did not undermine the spirit and the determination of the students. Ignoring the Principal's plea, they began *charkha* classes.[32] The *charkha* association was opened under the aegis of the Social Service League of the Students' Union. By 1944, it had acquired ten *charkhas,* five of which were bought by the Students' Union and the other five donated by the teachers.

All symbols and representations of British power seemed to provoke the students. They had even demanded the removal of the British vice chancellor, Sir Maurice Gwyer, organizing demonstrations and processions to insist on his removal. The Government reacted by police repression, teargas, and the use of bullets. Three students of the University were also suspended for their 'radicalism and activism'. The suspension of these students further incited the students. To express their anguish and anger against the Government, they organized demonstrations, *hartals*, and courted arrest, shouting slogans such as *Angrez Bharat Chodo*.[33]

A noteworthy development in women's participation in the national movement was the formation of the Mahila Atmaraksha Samiti, or Women's Self-defence League, popularly known as MARS, in 1942. The left wing women responsible for its formation included Kamala Chatterjee, Manikuntala Sen, Renu Chakravarty, and Ela Reid. MARS grew rapidly in Bengal. It participated in nationalist activities and also played a big role in relief work during the famine in Bengal.[34] In a similar spirit, the Delhi Women's League, a branch of the All India Women's Conference (AIWC) demanded civil liberties, preservation of freedom and the release of national leaders. The League urged AIWC to sanction its demands. AIWC, on the other hand, was not even prepared to move the motion put forth by the League, alleging that their demands sounded like a political gimmick. However, despite the initial resistance, the motion was tabled and passed in 1942 itself, with the support of Sarojini Naidu. This incident soured relations between the Delhi Women's League and the AIWC. The League broke away from AIWC and formed a new unit called Delhi Mahila Sangh—left-oriented in its approach but not affiliated to the communist party. Several girls from Indraprastha College were members. Of these, Sarla Sharma played a leading role in the association's activities. She was the general secretary of the Sangh while Begum Hashmi (grandmother of People's Theatre Movement leader Safdar Hashmi) was its President. The membership of the Sangh was open to all women irrespective of their political leanings. The attempt was to reach the masses through speeches and inter-active cultural programmes. By organizing such activities, Delhi Mahila Sangh made women aware of the political situation and the importance of civil liberties, Hindu–Muslim unity, proper rationing of food, de-hoarding and relief work for the Bengal famine. Since the Sangh had snapped its relations with AIWC, its *jalsas* or meetings were held in the houses of its members. In conversation with us, Sarla Sharma recalled nostalgically the contributions of Anwari Begum and Jamila Ustani, who were ever eager to host the *jalsas* of the Delhi Mahila

Sangh.[35] Parwati Didwania was yet another radical woman who adamantly stood by her values, remaining a loyal member of the Sangh despite family pressures. She, like many other women of those times gave up wearing jewellery and when her family objected to it, she wore jewellery but refused to miss a single meeting of the Delhi Mahila Sangh.[36]

Saheli Sabha was yet another centre or unit that engaged the girls of Indraprastha College. The objective of this organization was to bring together women from all sections of the society to discuss the national situation and spread the message of communal harmony amongst them so that they could foster it.[37] Saheli Sabha not only provided an avenue for the exchange of political opinions amongst women but also had a social purpose. It served as a medium for selling handicrafts made by poor, needy women. Two major exhibitions and sales that Saheli Sabha organized were at Purdahbagh (behind Jama Masjid) in 1953 and 1960 respectively. The former was christened Dastkari Mela and the latter Meena Bazar.[38]

REACTIONS TO THE EVENTS OF 1945

Nineteen forty-five was the year of the INA trials and the release of the national leaders arrested in 1942 during the Quit India Movement.[39] The INA had been a constant irritant to the British Government and as the Second World War approached its end, it got the opportunity it had been waiting for, to question members of the INA. The trial was held at Red Fort in Delhi for Generals Shah Nawaz, Gurdial Singh Dhillon, and Prem Sehgal, who had earlier been officers in the British Indian Army. They were accused of being traitors, of breaking their oath of loyalty to the British Government. In the course of the trial, the Government tried to paint the women INA members as weak and helpless, coerced into joining the INA. This was belied by the conduct and appearance of the women INA members at the trial—they looked heroic in full uniform as they saluted smartly and proudly declared themselves members of the Rani of Jhansi regiment of the INA. Only a few of the women members could return to India, and they were hailed by Indians as national heroes along with their male counterparts.[40]

Demonstrations and processions were organized throughout the country to demand the release of the INA soldiers—both men and women. Joining the countrywide movement, the students of different colleges in Delhi University also organized meetings and demonstrations to demand the release of the INA prisoners. Sameeruddin Khan, a student of St. Stephen's college (1945–47), disrupted the morning assembly in his college, mobilized students to boycott classes, organized a protest march and pulled down the Union Jack from the flagstaff.[41] In the same spirit, some students of Indraprastha College organized and led processions, joined by most of the girls of the college, singing the popular INA song *Kadam Kadam Badhaye Ja*. Caught in the midst of such intense political feeling, the Government could not ignore public opinion, at least in the case of INA prisoners. Thus, even though the court martial held them guilty, the Government decided to liberate them, evoking unprecedented public response as the nation celebrated the release of the INA prisoners.[42]

Even as the nation rejoiced over the liberation of the INA soldiers, there was more good news: the national leaders, arrested during the Quit India Movement, were set free in 1945. To welcome the leaders, a huge public rally was organized at the Ramlila Grounds in Delhi. The meeting was scheduled to be addressed by Jawaharlal Nehru, Maulana Azad, Sarojini Naidu, Sardar Patel, and Asaf Ali. The jubilant girls of Indraprastha College planned to attend the meeting. But, as Sucharita Sen Gupta, a student of the college in 1945, recounts, when the students came out of the college to go to Ramlila Grounds, they found to their dismay that no conveyance was available. Determined to reach the meeting at any cost, they walked all the way to the venue.[43]

Women in IPTA

The events of 1942 and 1945 infused the nation with an even greater resolve to oust the British from power. Amongst the various forms and methods adopted to express anger against the Government, IPTA (Indian Peoples Theatre Association) was a noteworthy one. Between 1943 and 1947, IPTA performed shadow plays and pantomimes with contemporary themes, with the purpose of attacking the British Government. IPTA was a voluntary body with no financial resources and yet it performed creditably. Their sets were simple—one *takht* (wooden bed) and white saris served as props. Several students of Indraprastha College, particularly those who were members of AISF, joined IPTA. Since the IPTA plays were aimed against the Government, the latter missed no opportunity to keep them away from the public or criticize them. It disallowed IPTA the use of posters and microphones to propagate their plays or the venues at which they were performed. Accepting the challenge, AISF mobilized college students through the Cultural Secretary of the Students' Unions of different colleges and urged the students to watch the IPTA plays and participate in IPTA activities. To reach out to larger groups of people, especially in the absence of posters and microphones, the IPTA members would write out the plays' titles and venues on newspapers and pasted them on the roads to publicize the events. Sarla Sharma, an active IPTA member, was responsible for the publicity in Chandni Chowk, the area that she lived in. When we interviewed her, she described how she and her friends used black pens to write on the newspapers to make posters and pasted them on the roads leading to the Yamuna river. As people traversed the roads on their way to the river for their morning baths, they would read them and perhaps attend the performances. IPTA's activities, supported by the students and the people of Delhi, truly represented people's power against the Government.

Women Power in the Mounting Freedom Struggle

In the midst of growing resistance, the British Government, in March 1946, sent the Cabinet Mission to India to negotiate with the Indian leaders the terms for the transfer of power to India. In October 1946, an interim cabinet led by Jawaharlal Nehru, comprising members from both the Congress and the Muslim League, was formed. But the elation of imminent independence was marred by the communal riots that rocked the nation during and after August 1946. Gandhi toured East Bengal and Bihar on foot to check the riots and appeal for peace. Several Hindus and Muslims sacrificed their lives to extinguish communalism. Women of all castes and class, emphasizing the notion of 'universal womanhood', which rejected the division of caste, class, party, and religion, also joined the struggle against communalism and partition.[44] Women from the AISF, including some students from Indraprastha College, went to jail for their activities. They were detained without trial and kept with the criminals. However, no fears or provocation could hinder their bold and courageous resolve to struggle. Sarla Sharma was one of the 24 women detained in Delhi jail without trial. When we talked to her, she expressed no complaints for the manner in which she was treated in the prison, only pride at the unified determination of Indians at that time to fight for the nation's independence. Sharma told us that it was not necessary to be aligned to any party or group or ideology in those days. Instead, it was important to possess and display emotions and passions against the British Government and an adamant and indomitable will to free India.[45]

In 1946, the Students' Union of Indraprastha College joined the nation wide attempts to spread the message of communal harmony. The Entertainment Society of the Union celebrated both Diwali and Id with equal fervour and on both the occasions invited the academia of Delhi to attend the functions. In the same spirit, to emphasize the value and the importance of the two languages—Hindi and Urdu—the Social Service League of the Students' Union conducted classes for the children of the neighborhood to teach them both the languages. *Pradeep*, the annual college magazine carried several articles emphasizing communal harmony and appealing against communal killings and the partition.

We may remind ourselves, as we have mentioned earlier, that the teachers of the college in those days, at the time of their employment, had to assure the college authorities that they would not involve themselves in any national political activity. Despite this promise, the teachers could rarely abstain from joining the freedom struggle. In this respect, most remarkable was the support that the teachers enjoyed from the Principal. The example of Nirmala Sherjung, a lecturer in the college in 1946–47 would illustrate our point. Sherjung, a fighter and a revolutionary, told us that notwithstanding her assurances to the college, she participated in the processions and demonstrations in 1946–47. In one such procession, she was in the front row carrying a *mashal*. As the procession passed through the University, someone saw her and complained to the college authorities. The Principal, Bina DasGupta, questioned Sherjung, who (apprehensive of losing her job) denied having participated in the procession. The violation of the college discipline was considered so severely unpardonable that the Principal's inquiry was not deemed sufficient. Consequently, the college management committee began an inquiry against Sherjung. One of the members of the committee pointed out that the witness was a respectable person, and therefore the complaint was definitely correct. The Principal's rejoinder was that whatever the status of the complainant, it was Sherjung's testimony that was important.[46] Such was the understanding and faith that the Principal and the teachers shared in those days.

FREEDOM, BUT AT WHAT COST?

Processions, demonstrations, appeals for communal harmony on one hand and atrocious instances of communalism on the other characterized the years 1946–47. Unprecedented killings and massacre tore the nation. India was on the verge of independence but the excitement, the happiness, the sense of glory associated with freedom was tainted with the communal carnage. Lord Mountbatten, who came to India as Viceroy in March 1947, worked out a compromise after long discussions with the leaders of the Congress and the Muslim League: India was to be free but not united. The country was partitioned, a new state of Pakistan was created, and India became free on 15 August 1947. The grief and pain of the killings and the partition undermined the joy and ecstasy. Gandhi, the messiah of peace and non-violence, toured the country, appealing for an end to manslaughter, but to no avail. Lakhs were uprooted from their ancestral land, compelled to make a choice between India and Pakistan. The editorial of *Pradeep*, published in May 1948 gives an insight into the sentiments of the young people at the time:

The world today seems to be in a sad turmoil ... with the international dissension widening into a yawning gulf ... with our own land having plunged in a ruinous state of affairs. Surely, this is the greatest crisis our country has ever faced...together we must strive and build up this beautiful land that is our home—yours and mine...'[47]

Jawaharlal Nehru addressed the Constituent Assembly on the night of 14 August 1947. Delhi University also made arrangements to celebrate the day of Independence and all the colleges were invited to join. The senior students of Indraprastha College, as of all the colleges of Delhi University, were taken to the Constituent Assembly to participate in the Independence Day celebrations. Apart from joining the collective festivities, Indraprastha College also organized a separate Independence Day function at the college and, like other public and official buildings, the college was illuminated at night. In tune with their feelings, the students on the day made financial contributions for the benefit of the refugees and presented the amount to the Government.

Delhi saw a huge influx of refugees. Refugee camps were set up in different parts of the city. The Social Service League of the Students Union of Indraprastha College responded with great maturity. The League organized stitching and knitting of garments for the refugees. Wool for the knitted garments was provided by the student-volunteers of the League as well as by the teachers. The teachers also provided 50 bundles of cloth from which the students could stitch more than 250 garments for the refugees. In an attempt to provide food relief to the refugee camps, the Social Service League requested the Principal for a plot of land within the college campus on which they could grow vegetables. On the land allotted by the Principal, the students grew potatoes, tomatoes, onions, spinach, and radish. Thus in their own small way, the students could make a contribution to the refugee centres.

The students' attempts to help the refugees included the organization of a fund called the Poor Fund to help the refugee students with books and miscellaneous items. Supported by the teachers the students organized a 'Fancy Fair', the proceeds of which were donated to the Prime Minister's Relief Fund for the benefit and betterment of the refugees. To inculcate feelings of communal amity and peace, the debating and the literary society of the Students' Union organized inter-college debates to propagate and generate communal harmony and a healthy understanding amongst the students of different educational institutions in Delhi.

The large increase in population after Partition changed the character of the city of Delhi and this had repercussions on the University as well. The University had to devise new rules to accommodate the displaced students from West Punjab. In 1947, immediately after Independence, classes in the second shift were opened in Indraprastha College, Hindu College, and Ramjas College. Indraprastha College catered solely to women students while Hindu and Ramjas College remained co-educational. According to the government plan, the classes in the second shift continued till 1949. The University understood that the second shift classes were just a temporary solution and that new colleges would have to be started to meet the demand. Hansraj College was started in 1947 as a co-educational college by the managing committee of DAV College in

Lahore. Punjab University volunteered to establish what was then called the Camp College. It employed several displaced teachers from colleges in West Punjab and the North-West Frontier Province. For almost a decade, Camp College continued to function from a number of buildings on Mandir Marg in Delhi. Later on, post-graduate classes of this college were taken over by Delhi University as an evening college and located in the Arts Faculty building. The undergraduate classes, over the years, were shifted to Nirmala College, managed by a Christian mission. Nirmala College was subsequently taken over by the Kirorimal Trust and renamed Kirorimal College in 1954.

NOTES AND REFERENCES

1. Interview with Sarla Sharma.
2. Ibid.
3. Kumari Jayawardene, *Feminism and Nationalism in the Third World*, p. 106.
4. Ibid.
5. Zohra Ansari was the daughter of M.A. Ansari, a staunch Congress worker and a Gandhian. She was subsequently married to Shaukatullah Ansari, the Governor of Orissa. Nafisa was the wife of Sultan Yar Khan, an advocate in Delhi.
6. Interview with Sarla Sharma.
7. Aruna Asaf Ali, *The Resurgence of Indian Women*, Radiant Publishers, New Delhi, 1991, pp. 136–7; Also see Sumit Sarkar, *Modern India*, Macmillan, New Delhi, 1998, p. 388.
8. Aruna Asaf Ali, *The Resurgence of Indian Women*, p. 136.
9. Sumit Sarkar, *Modern India*, pp. 389–91.
10. Aditya Bhattacharya, 'From An Ivory Tower', *The Stephanian*, Vol. LXXXVIII, No. I, Winter 1978–79, pp. 19–20.
11. Geraldine Forbes, *Women in Modern India*, p. 204.
12. Aparna Basu, 'The Role of Women in the Indian Struggle for Freedom', p. 31.
13. Reminiscences: Rup Seth, a student of the college in 1940–44.
14. Reminiscences: Pushpa Murgai, a student of the college in 1941–45.
15. Reminiscences: Vijaya Mehrotra, a student of the college in 1941–47.
16. Interview with Sarla Sharma.
17. Sunaina Sharma and Madhu Kishwar, 'Toofani Satyawati: An Unsung Hero of Freedom Struggle', p. 27.
18. Reminiscences: Kamla Mehta, a student of the college in 1939–43.
19. Aditya Bhattacharya, 'From An Ivory Tower'.
20. It was in 1924 in Lahore, the capital of undivided Punjab, that the Indian chapter of the Olympic Movement was born. The founder was G.D. Sondhi, the first Secretary of the Punjab Olympic Association. Lt. Col. H.L.O. Garrett, Vice

Principal of Government College, Lahore, was the president of the founder body. The same year, the country's first Olympic Games, now christened National Games, was organized in Lahore. The 10th edition of the Olympic Games was held in Patiala.

21. From the Superintendent of Education to the Chairman of the governing body of Indraprastha College, Letter No. 7335, 10 December, 1942 in Minutes of the governing body, 22 December, 1942.

22. Nirmala Sherjunj, 'Sharing Some Experiences', a talk given at the Indraprastha College Alumni Function, 10 February, 1998.

23. From J.C. Chatterjee, Education Department to the Secretary, Ramjas College (undated) in File—Miss K. Gupta, 24 March, 1939 to 3 March, 1943.

24. 'Preposterous? The 'No Wheat' Order', *The National Call*, 3 September, 1942.

25. Ibid.

26. 'Blessings', *The National Call*, 3 September, 1942.

27. Shanta Vashisht's interview in Nirmala Malhotra, 'Indraprastha College: Fifty Years of Women's Education', *Femina*, 10 May, 1974.

28. Sucharita Sen Gupta, 'Down the Memory Lane', in *The Golden Oriole, 1924–1974.*

29. Protima Mukerji, 'Looking Back', *Pradeep*, 1950 (a special issue on the occasion of the college's silver jubilee).

30. Nilima Chakravarty, 'My Views Regarding the College', *Pradeep*, 1950; Also Nirmala Prakash, 'Recalling the Past' in the same issue.

31. Nirmala Prakash, 'Recalling the Past'.

32. Ibid.

33. Sarla Sharma, 'Rashtriya Andolan Mein Indraprastha'.

34. Kumari Jayawardene, *Feminism and Nationalism in the Third World*, p. 106.

35. Anwari Begum was a widow with seven children, without any formal education. She had studied Urdu at home and had sufficient knowledge of it to write posters in Urdu and earn her living. Jamila Ustani, also a widow, lived in a one-room house for which she had to pay a sum of Rs 2.50. She taught Urdu and earned at least 12 annas per day by stitching 12 dozen buttons in a blouse. (Interview with Sarla Sharma).

36. Interview with Sarla Sharma.

37. Saheli Sabha was started by Akhtar Ara Begum (sister of the former President Fakhruddin Ali Ahmad), who was deeply committed to the issues of national and social welfare.

38. Chandrakanta Juneja, 'Tarashe Huae Aakar', in *The Golden Oriole, 1924–1974.*

39. INA or the Indian National Army or more popularly, the Azad Hind Fauj, was formed by Subhash Chandra Bose in Singapore in 1943 with the intention of securing the support of Japan to lead a campaign against Britain for the liberation of India. INA was joined in large numbers by the Indian residents in Southeast Asia and by Indian soldiers and officers captured by the Japanese forces in Malaya, Singapore, and Japan. Several Indian women had also joined the INA. In July 1943, Bose addressed the women's section of the Indian

Independence League of Singapore and exhorted them to join the Rani of Jhansi brigade of INA to fight as co-partners with men in the freedom struggle.

40. Geraldine Forbes, *Women in Modern India*, p. 214.
41. Aditya Bhattacharya, 'From An Ivory Tower'.
42. Sucharita Sen Gupta, 'Down the Memory Lane'.
43. Ibid.
44. Geraldine Forbes, *Women in Modern India*, pp. 221–2.
45. Interview with Sarla Sharma.
46. Nirmala Sherjung, 'Sharing Some Experiences'.
47. 'The Editorial', *Pradeep*, May 1948.

5

'New' Beginnings, Reorganization, and Reconstruction, 1940–47

Apart from being years of intense political activity for Indraprastha students, as for Indians in all parts of the country, the 1940s were also a period of significant changes in the functioning of the college, most of them occasioned by the restructuring and reorganization of Delhi University.

NEW BEGINNINGS

In 1939–40, particularly noticeable were some radical decisions and their implementation by Indraprastha College. As an example, we once again cite the case of Nirmala Sherjung, a lecturer in Psychology. Sherjung, although selected to teach Psychology was appointed in the Department of Philosophy. Psychology, in those days was not taught as a separate discipline. It was considered an integral part of Philosophy and was taught by teachers holding Masters degree in Philosophy. It was Indraprastha College which in 1939 took the initiative of appointing a qualified Psychology teacher to teach the subject. Other colleges soon followed the example.[1] The insistence on the specialization of the subject and that only those with required qualifications could be appointed as lecturers, had made its beginning in Delhi University.

Another landmark in the history of Indraprastha College was also associated with the year 1939 and with Nirmala Sherjung. Sherjung was the first married woman to be appointed as a lecturer in the college. Until then, only single women were appointed as lecturers, though there were three married men with families on the teaching staff. The rationale was that married women, with family obligations, would not be able to devote themselves to their profession and that if they went on maternity leave, it would disrupt the teaching work. A biased view indeed of a woman's potentialities and capabilities! And moreover a violation of the fundamental right of being a woman. Consequently, when Sherjung was appointed, there was a tacit understanding that she would not ask for maternity leave for quite sometime and that she would not let her domestic responsibilities interfere with her professional duties. Sherjung, in need of a job, gave her consent. But she was in a dilemma because she was pregnant. Finally, sure of being dismissed, she informed the Principal. To her astonishment, she found the Principal's response affectionate and understanding.[2] Sherjung could not only retain her job but continued to serve the college until her retirement in 1980. It established that the marital status of a woman could not determine her intellectual abilities or her sense of responsibility. It challenged gender bias: for if a married man could be sincere towards his profession so could a married woman.

We have noted in the earlier chapters the cautious approach of the college management in the appointment of lecturers. The lecturer to be appointed had to confirm that she would neither encourage nor participate in any political activity. Nirmala Sherjung, a CPI worker and a political activist, was asked to give a similar assurance. In need of a job, she complied. Her case is interesting: it was not only somewhat complex but also reflects a sense of understanding and trust that the college management had towards the teachers. Sherjung was married to a *krantikari* (political revolutionary), Chaudhury Sherjung, who after ten years of imprisonment was released in 1938, a year before Nirmala Sherjung's appointment to the college. He was externed from Punjab and was constantly shadowed by the police. Association with political revolutionaries, considered a menace at that time, was usually avoided. Rejecting such stigmas, Indraprastha College appointed Nirmala Sherjung on the condition as noted above. Barely a year after her appointment, in June 1940, her husband was again arrested under the Preventive Detention Act for an indefinite period. The reaction of the college significantly was not punitive but sympathetic. Instead of penalizing her for her husband's activities, the college management promptly provided her accommodation on the college premises, assuring her security against any unforeseen adversity.[3]

These developments came at a time when Indraprastha College was in the midst of reorganization, a process begun after its affiliation to Delhi University and subsequent to its shift in Alipur House. In November 1940, the Secretary of the governing body initiated the task of preparing a comparative statement of grades of salaries in force at colleges in other parts of India, particularly women's colleges. It may be interesting to note that the comparison of salaries was undertaken at a time when the salaries of men and women lecturers were not equal despite their similar qualifications and job. The grades of women lecturers in colleges in different parts of India were ascertained to be: Rs 125-5-175 for Junior Lecturer and Rs 175-10-250 for Senior Lecturer. The Junior Grade in Indraprastha College as fixed in 1936 was the same as in other colleges but there was a difference in the Senior Grade, which was fixed at Rs 150-10-200 in Indraprastha College. Realizing the vast discrepancies in salaries, the teachers demanded increments. The governing body was reluctant to grant any increments higher than those already sanctioned since there was no such provision in the budget of 1940–41. Nonetheless, it stipulated that if adequate provisions were made in the financial year 1941–42, it could consider a grant of conditional increment from April 1942, that is, only to those teachers who were given an increment of Rs 10 per month from October 1941. The governing body, it is apparent, made the decisions on the salaries and increments of the teachers although the college was affiliated to the University.

Another issue that agitated the teachers in 1940 was the maternity leave of R.W. Ghate, a lecturer in Economics. In the absence of any rules concerning maternity leave, the governing body advised the Honorary Secretary to obtain information on the rules regarding maternity leave from Lady Hardinge Medical College, Delhi, and the Government College at Lahore. This implied that unless these rules were ascertained, leave could not be granted to R.W. Ghate. It was a matter of concern that a college that hired the services of women had not devised rules to protect and secure their interests.

While the decisions on matters pertaining to salary, increments, and maternity leave of the teachers were still awaited, the college embarked on other items of reorganization with the aim of enhancing the academic environment of the college. Responding to Vice

Chancellor Maurice Gwyer's suggestion of making Delhi University a purely 'Honours' University, the governing body in 1940 began consultations on starting Honours classes in English, Economics, Philosophy and Sanskrit. In November 1940, a sub-committee was set up to study and review the financial implications of beginning Honours classes in the college. But prior to sanctioning the Honours classes, the sub-committee recommended the strengthening of the Department of English. With this objective, it suggested an additional grant to improve the library facilities for the English section. Acknowledging that the introduction of Honours classes could enhance the workload, the sub-committee recommended an increase in the teaching staff by appointing at least one teacher in the Department of English, capable of teaching Honours classes. Subject to the qualifications of the teacher, the sub-committee was even willing to consider an appointment in the Senior Grade. Following the recommendation, two new appointments were made in 1940 and 1941 for the teaching of English exclusively. In fact, in 1941, the governing body was considering an appointment of a lecturer in English at a higher salary, although not exceeding Rs 200, provided she also knew Hindi or Urdu. The stipulation on the knowledge of Hindi or Urdu was because translation was important in the teaching of English in those days.

As the college expanded, several other issues related to the interests of the teachers were raised. To build a consensus between the teachers and the governing body and for an amicable solution of problems, if any, the College Society Rules in 1941 made a provision that the Staff Council of the college would elect a member from the teaching staff as a member of the governing body for a period of three years. The first nominee of the Staff Council to the governing body, in June 1941 was Roma Dasgupta Nee Sircar, a lecturer in History. The year 1941 was also significant for the governing body's decision to institute the office of a vice-principal. Some members of the governing body argued that the rapid growth in the number of students necessitated the appointment of a Vice-Principal. They suggested that a member from the teaching staff could be appointed as a Vice-Principal for a period, to be decided by the governing body on the recommendation of the Principal, who may previously consult her staff.

The expansion of the college entailed additions to the teaching faculty and reorganization at different levels, enhancing the financial liabilities of the college. In such circumstances in 1940, it became necessary to raise the tuition fee from Rs 9 to Rs 10 per month for the intermediate classes although the fees for undergraduate degree classes was continued at Rs 12 as fixed in 1937. To counter the financial problems, the Board of Trustees suggested stipends for poor students. It appealed to private, wealthy persons, who had pledged commitment to uplifting their castes, for funds. The first response came from Lala Shankar Lal of Delhi Cloth and General Mills Limited, Delhi. In 1940, he offered four merit-cum-means scholarships of Rs 10 each to Vaish Aggarwal girls who passed the University examinations in the First Division but were too poor to pursue further studies. Similarly, Mrs Sultan Singh, wife of a former member of the governing body, donated a sum of Rs 132 for two scholarships in 1942. These were to be granted to either Jain or Vaish Aggarwal girls. One was to be given to a student of Preparatory or II year class (Rs 5 per month) while the other was to be granted to a student of III year or IV year class (Rs 6 per month).

The college management scrutinized all avenues that could contribute to stabilizing the finances of the college. Towards this end, the management proposed the formation of an Old Students Association. The former students, it was argued, could prove to be a perennial source of strength for the college because as future mothers, they would think of Indraprastha College for the education of their daughters. Secondly, their old links could compel them to disburse some charity towards their alma mater. The proposal, although rational in its conception, could not be enforced immediately. It took a few years for the idea to be concretized and the Old Students Association to become active.

As it moved ahead in identifying the growing needs of an expanding institution, the management recognized the importance of a canteen in the college. A canteen was necessary for both the teachers and the students, especially when they had long hours of stay in college. A maid called Katto had filled the vacuum of a canteen since 1927: she would escort the girls from their homes to college in the college bus and once in college, she cooked delicious food for them. The students of those days remember her and her anecdotes with great fondness. She would discuss the war with them and knew that the war was being fought 'between the white men and Hitler' but her sole worry was how and from where she would bring *atta* (flour) to feed the students.[4] The girls of that bygone era remember

her as a 'second mother of the alma mater.'[5] It was to complement
the efforts of Katto that the idea of the canteen was proposed in
1942. On this issue the college management was pleasantly surprised
by the philanthropy of a private individual, Sahdev Sondhi from
Jullundur. He volunteered to donate the entire cost of the construction
of the canteen in March 1942, in memory of his wife, Dayawanti
Sondhi, though on certain conditions. First, he insisted that the
construction of the canteen should be completed within a month
and second, the rent charged from the 'Restaurant' (that is what he
decided to call the canteen) should be paid as scholarship to the
poor and deserving students. The conditional financial support came
as a boon to the college for it needed both—a canteen as well as
scholarships for its students. The construction of the 'Restaurant',
more popularly the canteen, was completed by April–May 1942.

INDRAPRASTHA HOSTEL UNDER SCRUTINY

In the process of reorganization and expansion, the admission policy
of the college was quite clear—it practiced no bias against any
community, caste, or religion. However, the plural character of the
college failed to convince at least some sections in Delhi society.
They alleged that the college was prejudiced against a certain
community in making admissions to the hostel. The Delhi Provincial
Students Federation complained that non-Hindu girls were not
admitted to the hostel. The governing body conceded that though a
few non-Hindu girls were refused admission to the hostel, their religion
and faith were not the reason. The scarcity of space caused problems
in the kitchen and dining room for cooking and serving non-vegetarian
food. This appears to be an unconvincing argument for not admitting
non-Hindu and non-vegetarian students to the hostel. But, in the
Indian society of those days, when social as well as food habits were
extremely rigid, vegetarians may have had objections to dining with
non-vegetarians, as the example of Razia Sultana, admitted to the
hostel in May 1941, would vouchsafe. Special arrangements were
made for cooking her food and serving it in her room. A hostel
employee, Nasiruddin, was instructed to serve food in her room and
she was asked to pay Rs 4 per month for this extra service. Razia
followed this practice for a fortnight but then applied to the governing
body, demanding that she be allowed to eat in the dining room with
the other girls. The governing body considered her application only

to reiterate that food would continue to be served in her room. Challenging the decision, Razia neither obeyed the strictures of the governing body nor did she pay Nasiruddin. She ate in the dining room with the other girls. Razia's defiance is noteworthy. She obviously did not wish to be isolated or treated differently from her peer group. Her behaviour can be used as an example to explain the growing assertiveness, independence, and sense of dignity and identity that women were acquiring, irrespective of their caste or faith. It is difficult to suggest whether she agreed to eat vegetarian food. But in the given circumstances, when casteism and food habits were rigidly enforced, it can be conjectured that she must have had vegetarian food. Non-vegetarian food cooked in the same kitchen with vegetarian food or served along with it was inconceivable in those days.

The issue of the admission of non-Hindu girls to the Indraprastha College hostel continued to provoke controversy. To garner public support on the matter, the Delhi Provincial Students Federation actively used the media.[6] Equally emphatically, the college authorities reiterated the egalitarian nature of the admission policy and that the major problem was the lack of space to provide separate dining rooms for vegetarian and non-vegetarian students. Temporary arrangements were made to suit the different food habits of the students, with no intentions of hurting the sentiments of any community. The secretary defended this pattern, arguing that it would continue until sufficient funds and building material were made available to make additions to the hostel block.[7]

The hostel was again in the midst of a controversy in the latter months of the 1940s. As a result of the war, prices had soared and despite government control, they could not be restored to their normal value even by the late 1940s. The Principal of the college reported the growing difficulties of the hostel in meeting the kitchen and other expenses. Yet she was not willing to consider increasing the hostel fees. Instead, she recommended the adjustment and control of expenses. On the other hand, the hostel students, ignorant or perhaps overlooking the financial strains, demanded fee concession for a fortnight in December 1940 during the Christmas vacations. When the Principal and the secretary of the governing body rejected their demand, they threatened to go on hunger strike. The secretary attempted to pacify them, arguing that the matter would have to be referred to the governing body. He succeeded in persuading the students to pay half the fees. Significantly, the students also agreed to pay the other half of the fees in January if the governing body refused to grant fee concession for the Christmas vacations.

The rebellion of the students was not confined to matters of fees. They also raised their voice against some hostel rules, particularly those pertaining to their outings, which they found to be a curb on their independence. The resentment of the students was widely reported in various newspapers. Of special interest is the news item entitled 'Educational Reform' in *The Hindustan Times*. It was reported that the matron escorted the hostelers to the Yamuna river at Bela Road and that they often returned in wet clothes.[8] The report agitated the governing body of the college. Fearing that such reports might adversely affect the image of the college, the governing body admonished the Principal, questioning the propriety of these visits and their effect on the health of the students. Understanding the independent and fun-loving attitude of the young girls, the Principal supported the students. She explained to the governing body that such walks to the river were not a rarity—the students, accompanied by teachers, often went to the river, and sometimes would playfully walk into the water, wetting the edges of their saris. She argued that this behaviour was neither indecent nor injurious to health. Emboldened by the Principal's support, the students ventured to express their opinion on the issue. The Hostel Union passed a resolution in December 1941 insisting that the hostel students should be allowed to go out without their teachers provided there were more than two girls. This resolution, during the evolving years of the college, reflects the change in the attitude of the students, their desire for more freedom

REORGANIZATION OF DELHI UNIVERSITY

Indraprastha College's efforts at revitalization coincided with the demand of the vice chancellor of Delhi University, Sir Maurice Gwyer, to the government to implement his scheme of reorganization of Delhi University. The central government accepted the vice chancellor's proposal in February 1940 and with this the reorganization of the colleges affiliated to Delhi University was also initiated. Maurice Gwyer had visions of creating an all-India University in Delhi that would attract students of all categories—graduates and post-graduates—from all parts of India. He argued that the establishment of provincial autonomy and the complete provincialization of education had necessitated a university of this kind in Delhi. A provincial University, he observed, reflected and focused on the cultural life of a province but the university at the centre would be an all-India cultural centre representing a wider and more general outline. It would, to quote Maurice Gwyer, 'become a clearing house of ideas and of intellectual progress; and it might profoundly influence those who may in future become responsible for the Government of India.'[9] The vice chancellor submitted a memorandum to the Government deploring the condition of the University as it existed in 1942 and proposing reforms. The University then did not possess a single Professor. The reason obviously was the lack of funds and therefore the inability of the University to establish professorial chairs. Moreover, only two Science subjects—Physics and Chemistry—were taught but their learning was confined only to the level of BSc Pass. The library, most adversely affected by scanty funds, was a discredit to the University. And, above all, the University buildings were in complete shambles. To keep the University alive as an institution of which neither the capital nor the country would be ashamed, Maurice Gwyer made the following proposals: transfer of all colleges except Indraprastha College (it had already made a shift to Alipur House, which was approximately 4 km from the University, a distance deemed reasonable to be considered within the University campus) to the University site; introduction of a three-year BA degree course; creation of an adequate number of chairs for Professors and Readers; extending the teaching of Science subjects to the Honours level; provision of scholarships; facilities for Post-graduate studies; establishment of a Medical faculty; organizing playfields and physical training; enforcement of statutes relating to the independent status of the recognized colleges; review of the conditions of government grants to the colleges; and encouraging students from other Indian states to join Delhi University. He also proposed that 'if possible allow only such persons to enter who were prepared to read for an Honours degree'.[10]

To facilitate the scheme, the central government decided to make a non-recurring grant to Delhi University, subject to the vote of the legislative assembly. Of the total sum, approximately half was to be used to assist the colleges to move to the University site. The intention was that all colleges except Indraprastha College should move to the University campus. Grants from the Government for this purpose were conditional, with the colleges themselves raising a substantial part of the total sum required.[11]

Apart from the non-recurring grant, the Government also increased the recurring grant to the University, but again subject to the approval of the legislative assembly. The recurring grant, it was argued, would facilitate the University in initiating a scheme for the appointment of professors, readers and post-graduate research scholars in such subjects as the University may deem necessary. The proposal of reorganization by the vice chancellor led many a time to agitated exchanges between him and the governing bodies and the trustees of the colleges of Delhi University, who feared the curtailment of their privileges in case the University exerted its powers and insisted on uniformity in all its colleges.

Gwyer's recommendation of the introduction of a three-year degree course from the beginning of the academic session in 1943 would, he realized, necessitate the reorganization of the Secondary School system in Delhi. The Government had already made a grant for this purpose. However, to prevent any difficulties for the students, the vice chancellor conceded the continuance of the preparatory classes until secondary education was thoroughly overhauled. He urged that Delhi University should take a lead in the reorganization of degree classes without waiting for the older universities to come to a decision. The syllabuses for three-year degree courses in BA and BSc Pass and Honours streams were devised by the concerned faculties and sanctioned by the Academic Council and the Executive Council in April 1943. The Delhi University Act was amended in 1943 to provide for three-year BA degree courses.[12] The Act of 1943 also made a provision for a full-time paid vice chancellor, who would serve a term of 5 years and was not eligible for reappointment. These provisions, however, did not apply to Gwyer himself. This man of vision and strong convictions had a long, successful, reformist stint of 12 years as the vice chancellor of Delhi University.[13]

The University was on the path of transformation. But the federal scheme of the University could not be effectively implemented unless all men's colleges moved to the University site, otherwise no plan for co-operative teaching would be feasible. St. Stephen's College had shifted to its new site (where it now stands) and the building of Hindu College was in the process of completion. It was conjectured that the other colleges would start construction as soon as the prices of building materials (highly inflated due to the Second World War) were restored to their normal value.[14] Very soon, several other colleges were established under Delhi University's patronage. It was certain that once the regulations of the University were ascertained all the colleges affiliated to Delhi University would have to abide by them.

One of the aspects Gwyer had touched upon in his programme of reform and reorganization was the teacher–student relationship, stressing the need for a better rapport and communication between the two. Regretting the negligible influence of the teachers on the students, Maurice Gwyer emphasized the essentials of personal contact in any system of education and most of all in University education. He suggested that this could be effectively achieved by creating autonomous societies within the University, each making itself responsible for a limited number of students.[15] Indraprastha College authorities were willing to accept this proposal of the vice chancellor although they claimed that a close association between the teachers and students of the college already existed, as did the intense involvement of both in the activities of the college. However, the college management was upset by the vice chancellor's scheme of the reconstitution of the governing bodies of the colleges. Gwyer was prepared to concede to the idea of independent and autonomous governing bodies provided the nature of the bodies could be changed. He argued that according to the report of the Bhatnagar Committee of Inspection, only two colleges had funds of their own that they exclusively used for their own purposes. The other colleges were maintained by trusts or societies that had a group of undertakings to support and that they often appropriated funds out of a common pool to meet the requirements of their undertakings. The financial position of such colleges, the vice chancellor alleged, was precarious and uncertain and thus they had no independent position. Indraprastha College was one such college.[16] The college management rejected the observations of the vice chancellor. Regretting the response of Indraprastha College, Maurice Gwyer stipulated that for receiving government grants, it would be obligatory for the colleges to reorganize themselves as independent and autonomous units. The reorganization scheme necessitated the representation of both the University and the teaching staff on the governing bodies of colleges. Despite the opposition of colleges like Indraprastha College, Maurice Gwyer did not abandon his efforts at convincing them that institutions which spent large sums of public money—and no college could sustain itself without government grants and students' fees, both of which were public money—should have a more public and representative character.[17]

A long dialogue ensued between the vice chancellor and the management of Indraprastha College on this issue. The Honorary Secretary of the governing body of the college opined that some of Gwyer's conditions would destroy the self-contained character of the institutions and their spirit of independence. Objecting vehemently to the vice chancellor's suggestion of the abolition of the Board of Trustees in the college, he argued that almost all the trustees were founders who had made unprecedented contributions in the form of money and labour for the development of the college. One may not object, he argued, to such representation of the University and the teaching staff on the governing bodies as demanded by the scheme but to deprive the founders, supporters and sponsors of an effective voice in the management would result in the deterioration of the college. Moreover, the proposal of a tighter government control over the accounts and the investments of the college may result in a reduced income for the college. The secretary argued that the situation would be further aggravated by the rule which prescribed that the government grant would be conditional upon obtaining a certificate from the vice chancellor that the requisite terms have been duly fulfilled by the recipient. Apprehending complete erosion of power of the college management, the secretary expressed his opposition to yet another condition, that is, that no college would be allowed to make any appointment or dismiss any member of the teaching staff without the prior permission of the University. In such an event, the secretary feared, there could be an undesirable canvassing at the time of appointment and dismissal of teachers. The Secretary's views reflected the concerns of all the members of the governing body and the trustees. To make his arguments more convincing, the secretary gave them a legalistic tone by suggesting that some of the measures of the vice chancellor might go against the authority of the Executive Council without the modification of the statute or amendment of the University Act itself.[18] In one of his letters to the vice chancellor, the secretary regretted that the conditions attached to the new scheme were so 'onerous, discouraging and impracticable.'[19] Further, he argued that under the present circumstances with almost all the institutions facing the brunt of war conditions, it was impossible to garner enthusiasm and resources for the successful working of the scheme of development as postulated by the Government or the vice chancellor.[20]

Sir Maurice Gwyer was prompt with his rejoinder. He accused the secretary of the management committee of Indraprastha College of misunderstanding his proposals. The vice chancellor denied the allegations of having ever suggested the abolition of the Board of Trustees. His scheme instead, he reiterated, was for the reconstitution of such bodies to give them a more public and a representative character. He denied that it was ever propossed that the University and the college teaching staff would have a large representation on the governing body of any college. With regard to the college accounts, the suggestions were that they should be kept in the form prescribed by the Government and that the auditors approved by the Government should audit them. There was no plan, the vice chancellor stipulated, to deprive the college of its money or reduce its income. In fact, it was adequately defined that the investments belonging to the colleges—all of which would necessarily be trust money—would be kept in trustee securities. In Maurice Gwyers opinion, no 'well-managed institution' could possibly object to these proposals. Regarding the scheme of appointment and dismissal of teachers also, the vice chancellor expressed his astonishment at the complaints of the secretary. He insisted that while there was no plan to deprive the governing bodies of their privilege to appoint or dismiss teachers, the University would have a right of veto on an appointment if in its opinion the appointment were an 'undesirable one'.[21] The vice chancellor, through his many letters, correspondences and meetings, hoped to convince the colleges affiliated to Delhi University of the value of his plan of reorganization. However, once it was ready to be implemented, the colleges had very little option but to accept it and abide by it, even though they may not have been favourably inclined towards it.

At the end of May 1942, the vice chanceller ordered all the colleges affiliated to Delhi University to reconstitute their governing bodies as a preliminary to receiving government grants. He argued that colleges that received grants of public money could not retain a private or a quasi-private status and that it was obligatory for the governing bodies of all colleges to have a more public and a representative character. As regards teachers, he reiterated that the aim was to secure to every teacher her/his scale of salary and regular increments. No increments to the teachers could be withheld without the consent of the

University—this would ensure uniformity in all colleges as well as justice for teacher. The vice chancellor also urged upon the governing bodies the maintenance of a Provident Fund for teachers in accordance with the rules prescribed by the University. To ensure that the allocated funds were not misappropriated, he specified that the University auditor would annually audit the accounts. The vice chancellor stressed the urgent need for the colleges and their governing bodies to comply with all the relevant statutes, ordinances, and regulations of the University. The vice chancellor's scheme gave the University a fresh direction, sparking a process of evolution and development that provided Delhi University a new and a permanent shape.

  The period also witnessed other new proposals for universities, including Delhi University, that promised new hope for the future of education. In 1945, there was a proposal to establish a University Grants Commission whose function would be to distribute government grants to the different Universities and coordinate the Government's efforts at developing education. This suggestion aroused several apprehensions. One of them was that the establishment of such a commission might interfere with the autonomy of the universities. Maurice Gwyer, however, disagreed with such fears. He argued that autonomy is purchased at too high a price if for example it implies freedom to neglect the interests of the University teachers. Convinced of the utility of the University Grants Commission, the vice chancellor stipulated that the government grants should always be welcomed as indispensable and necessary for the sustenance of the universities. Maurice Gwyer was willing to concede the benefits and importance of private endowments but he was adamant in his view that these endowments could produce a better impact and be more effective if combined with government grants.[22] At his speech at the Convocation of 1946 Gwyer emphasized the need to give adequate salaries to teachers for a healthy environment and diligent imparting of knowledge in the Universities.[23] The teacher, as he often said, is 'the kingpin of the education system'. The teachers of Delhi University, even then, were paid salaries higher than elsewhere in India. Consequently, it could attract good teachers. A teacher appointed in any of the constituent colleges was deemed a university teacher for the purpose of service conditions, pay scales, and various other perks enjoyed by teachers directly appointed by the University.[24] Influenced by Gwyer's ardent support of the interests of the teachers and their role and contribution in the sphere of education, the University of

Delhi in 1945 decided that each college should have two teachers as representatives on the governing body—one representing teachers who had served the college for more than 10 years and the other from amongst those who had served it for less than 10 years.[25] Maurice Gwyer's contributions can indeed be counted as significant, with a lasting impact on the structure of Delhi University.

RESPONSES TO THE NEW SCHEME OF DELHI UNIVERSITY

The responses to the proposed regulations for Delhi University were varied. In March 1942, the governing body of Indraprastha College informed the University of its decision to enforce new scales of salaries for its teachers from 1 April 1943 with certain conditions and limitations. In those days, since there was a distinction in the salaries of men and women teachers, the members of the governing body suggested that the scales of salaries of women teachers would be four-fifths of the full grade given to the men teachers. But, the members also submitted a memorandum to the Educational Advisor to the Government to sanction equal scales of salaries for both men and women teachers: since this would involve heavy capital expenditure, it was necessary for the University to ensure that the Government would provide the required funds by way of non-recurring grants. The managing committee further stated that to extend women's education as widely as possible under the new scheme, a considerable number of scholarships and other concessions might be necessary. The committee, therefore, suggested that apart from the government grant of 50% to meet the enhanced salaries of the teachers, the Government should also make a grant to facilitate the management's contribution to the teachers' Provident Fund, leave allowances paid to the teachers, and salaries to the administrative staff. The committee also demanded an increase in the grant for general expenditure from 20% to 40%, without which, it argued, it would be impossible to meet the growing needs of the expanding college.

The college management advanced yet another view on the issue of the fixing of salaries. It suggested that as the constituent colleges of Delhi University offered various courses of study at different levels, a uniform standard of salaries for their teachers appeared neither advisable nor practical. The committee argued, for instance, that the standard of salaries in colleges teaching BA (Honours) and MA should be higher than that of those teaching BA (Pass). This argument of the management committee seems illogical: teachers who taught BA (Pass) and those who taught BA (Honours) and MA could not be distinguished on the basis of their academic qualifications and pursuits. Moreover, the BA (Honours) and MA courses were in the process of being introduced in all the colleges of Delhi University. And, even if they were not, the teachers could not be punished for it, since they had all been appointed on the basis of the desired and required standards of merit laid down by the University. In fact, equality in salaries, irrespective of the gender and the courses taught by the teachers, were the only ways of ensuring uniformity and healthy relationships in the university's teaching environment. However, it seems such arguments were not recognized by the management committee of Indraprastha College in 1942 in its suggestions of distinctions in the salaries of teachers teaching BA (Pass), BA (Honours), and MA and creation of an intermediate grade between the Senior and the Junior grades of teachers proposed by the University. The committee also proposed that, since the work of the Principals in the BA (Pass) colleges would not be the same as in the colleges with BA (Honours) and MA, the salaries of the Principals of the former colleges should not be as high as the latter ones. The management committee further urged that in order to keep the recurring expenses of the college within reasonable limits, the proportion of students to teachers should be raised from 20:1 to 25:1. It observed that Indraprastha College had fulfilled the prescribed norms for the government grant. In fact, the committee argued, in pursuance of the new scheme, the college had decided to limit the number of students on the college roll to 500.

While appearing to make efforts to conform with the new plan, the management of Indraprastha College continued with strategy of bargaining with the University and the Government. For instance, the Honorary Secretary of the governing body expressed to the vice chancellor the inability of the management to change the name of the college at the present stage of its development. The college was then called Indraprastha Girls' College. While there is no evidence to establish the co-relation between the change in the name of the college and the development plans, it may be surmised that it was a way to warn the University that the management was in no hurry to change the constitution of the college as per the new plan. Our conjecture is based on a letter written by a member of the governing body, Dr Ram Kishore, to Maurice Gwyer. While Dr Kishore conveyed the satisfaction of the governing body over the decision of the University to grant the entire management of the administrative and financial matters of the college to the governing body, he urged upon the vice chancellor to reconsider the status of the Board of Trustees. Dr Kishore insisted that the Board of Trustees should be continued in 'some recognized position for sentimental reasons' else it might disrupt their 'deep-rooted feelings.'[26] Dr Ram Kishore also brought the financial status of the college to the notice of the vice chancellor. He pointed out that the revised scales of salaries of teachers were dependent on the government grants. Therefore, if at any time, the government grants were withdrawn, either wholly or partially, the college would not feel obliged to pay increased salaries to the teachers.[27] The financial resources of the college were so scanty that even though the salaries of the teachers were enhanced, the burden of the new courses could not be borne. Accordingly, the introduction of BA (Honours) and MA and the teaching of Punjabi as a vernacular language were deferred in early 1943 to a date to be decided by the management committee subject to the availability of funds.

Ignoring the objections and the suggestions of the managing committee of Indraprastha College, the vice chancellor emphasized the fulfillment of two other conditions of the new scheme— replacement of men teachers by women teachers and an assurance that no men teachers would be appointed in future and that the appointment of a new Principal would be according to the norms set by the University. This caused much resentment: the secretary asserted that if the college submitted meekly, several other demands of the vice chancellor would follow 'till we shall be to all intents and purposes treated as foreigners in our own temples of learning.'[28] He regretted that through such unfair and irrational proposals, the Government ensured 'peaceful penetration' into the colleges to change them 'into so many factories for producing slaves'.[29] He described his comments as 'the effusions of a disgruntled soul who is out to serve for freedom and not for slavery.'[30]

The college management nominated Dr Ram Kishore a member of the governing body, to represent the case of men teachers to the vice chancellor. Dr Kishore reported that the two men teachers of the college—G. Goswami who taught Mathematics and Bengali and Ramadeva who taught Sanskrit—had been on the teaching staff since the foundation of the college and that their work had always been satisfactory. Another member of the governing body, Begum Shah

Nawaz, remarked that it would be unfair on the part of the college to deprive these teachers of their jobs especially since they had served the college for 19 years. She argued that they had spent the best part of their lives in college and it would now be impossible for them to find employment elsewhere. Making a strong case for retaining the services of the two teachers, the Begum reiterated that even though Indraprastha College was a girls college, there was no harm in continuing the services of these teachers, particularly considering their age (they were about 50 years old).

The issue was resolved in favour of the men teachers and their services were retained. But, there was a sudden reversal of decision in January 1959 when the services of G. Goswami were discontinued without any warning. He was compelled to forfeit one-year's salary which amounted to more than Rs 8000, and the Principal B. Dasgupta was adamant about not paying him the gratuity. Goswami wrote to Lala Shriram, Chairman of the governing body of the college, expressing his anguish and sentiments towards the college: '... on October 5, 1925, Miss G'meiner received me with great regard and affection and appointed me a combined teacher of Maths, Science and Bengali ... I was one of the three teachers teaching eight girls only ... working hard for more than 15 years without any assistant. I organized and consolidated all the three departments of Maths, Science and Bengali ... the Principal Miss Dasgupta had assured me of extension and had said that Mr T.N. Zutshi is working here, though he is 78 years old with all the privileges of a lecturer... .'[31] By 1960, there were no men teachers on the teaching staff. They were removed either by arbitrary dismissal (G. Goswami), retirement (Ramadeva), or death (T.N. Zutshi). Since then, there have been no appointments of men on the teaching staff. Thus the college could implement this part of Gwyer's scheme, mostly by default.

Another aspect of the new scheme that proved difficult to implement in Indraprastha College in 1942–43 was the appointment of a highly qualified Principal. In fact, at the time of its recognition as a degree college, the college management had been instructed to appoint a Principal with high academic qualifications. The task of searching for such a Principal, to replace Kalavati Gupta, was initiated in August 1942. The post of the Principal advertised in August 1942 stipulated that the applicant should have secured a first class in MA (preferably in English) with wide administrative experience in a first-grade college. The Selection Committee, which met in August 1943, recommended two essential qualifications for the Principal viz. she should have been educated abroad or should have some educational experience in either a British or any other foreign University; secondly, she should have administrative experience of a degree college. Apart from the recommendations of the Selection Committee, the management committee of the college emphasized various other qualifications for the Principal. One of their specifications was that the Principal of such a college as Indraprastha should be a Hindu lady, who understands the sentiments, feelings, culture, and requirements of the students, majority of whom were Hindus.[32] This seems strange in view of the fact that the institution admitted girls from all communities, caste, and religion. Moreover, several members on the Governing Body of the college were Muslims and Christians. The answer, perhaps, can be found in the context of the society of those days. Since most of the donors and investors in the college endowment fund were Hindus and believers of Sanatan Dharma, it was probably necessary for the college management to emphasize the institution's Hindu character to sustain their support. That the management committee of the college was far from being reactionary, narrow-minded, or discriminatory is evident from yet another condition that the management laid down as a prerequisite for the post of the Principal. It insisted that the Principal should be a thorough nationalist and be able to command the respect and affection of her students irrespective of their religion, caste, or political ideas. Emphasizing the importance of nationalism and warning that the Principal should never become a tool in the hands of the British Government, the management committee expected the Principal not to discourage or suppress patriotism for the maintenance of discipline but to direct the political enthusiasm and feelings of the students into constructive channels, that is, develop in them a spirit of selfless service towards their families, communities, and the country. The management committee urged that while discipline should mean uninterrupted studies, it should not be used to create a false sense of loyalty to an alien government. In other words, the Principal should be like a guide to develop the physical, intellectual, moral, and spiritual strength of the Indian women rather than become a superintendent of a 'slave producing factory'.[33] To inculcate these qualities in the students, it was essential for the Principal to have a close rapport with the students. To achieve this, it was suggested that the Principal should teach at least one period a week in every class.[34] Subsequent to this preliminary discussion, the post of the Principal was offered to K.S. Ranga Rao.

With the appointment of the Principal according to the norms laid down by the new plan, Indraprastha College fulfilled most of the conditions as envisaged by the new scheme. Conscious of the necessity of following the new plan for receiving the government grant, the governing body of the college dissolved the then existing college society in August 1943 and registered itself as a new society in the name of Indraprastha College Women's Educational Trust. The governing body of the college was also registered as a separate legal entity. It was under these new provisions that the college changed its name to Indraprastha College for Women in September 1945. The change in the name of the college may not be significant in itself but the college had definitely matured and broadened its horizon and so had its girls. Sita Parmanand, the Principal of the college during 1945–47, commenting on the change said that the change in the name of the college was 'the most important fact to report in 1946'. The name Indraprastha Girls' College, she said, was a 'veritable tongue twister in the mouth of the people unfamiliar with English pronunciation and who insisted on giving it a vernacular air.'[35]

To ensure the release of the government grant to the college, the secretary of the governing body was prompt in informing the vice chancellor that the college had adopted the new scheme from 1 April 1943. However, the salaries of the teachers continued to be based on the old system: the governing body reiterated that the scheme of higher scale of salaries and dearness allowances for teachers could be implemented only if the government grant was sanctioned.

The persistent appeals of the governing body of Indraprastha College in 1943 for the government grant had some impact. The Government offered to provide finances for the payment of dearness allowance to the teachers. The teaching staff of the college was thus sanctioned an extra increment in December 1943. More significant, however, was the decision to fix the same salaries for both women and men teachers. The much-awaited gender equality, at least in the case of salaries, was finally achieved for the academia. It was indeed a radical decision for those times. Since then, University teachers have continued to enjoy this equality.

With the reorganization of Delhi University and a simultaneous reorientation of school education in Delhi, Indraprastha College faced a drastic decline in the number of students in the preparatory class in 1942–43. The apprehension was that the teachers associated with teaching the preparatory class might become surplus and may require retrenchment. Therefore, before the situation could turn into a crisis, the college management decided to absorb them into the different departments of the college. Only two teachers were assigned preparatory classes. Out of these, one of them was also allocated degree classes for the undergraduates. Consequently, no new appointments were made in the department of English. However, despite the reallocation of teaching work, the implementation of the new scheme added to the expenditure of the college. This entailed the enhancement of tuition fees. In April 1943, the fees were fixed at Rs 10 per month for the preparatory class and Rs 15 per month for the BA students. However, the college management remained sensitive to the needs and the interests of several students and made a provision for fee concession at Rs 12 per month for undergraduates if their parents earned less than Rs 500 per month. In the same spirit, it introduced stipends of two kinds in 1943—one for poor students, that is, a means scholarship at the rate of Rs 7 or Rs 8 per month and one for poor but academically deserving students, that is, a merit-cum-means scholarship at Rs 10 per month. For exceptionally deserving students (in academics) full remission of fees was granted if they could not afford to pay it. The Principal was also given the discretion to consider individual cases.

In 1945, Indraprastha College was engaged in equipping itself for the introduction of BA Honours and MA courses. Lala Shriram, chairman of the governing body of the college, eagerly pursued the cause of these courses. In Delhi University, in those days, joint lectures were held for all colleges for Honours and MA classes. Young women from orthodox Hindu and Muslim families were not permitted by their families to join these co-educational classes. With the introduction of these courses in Indraprastha College, many young women would be able to fulfil their dream of higher education. Towards this end, Lala Shriram made constant efforts to search for highly qualified teachers for the college to teach these courses. In 1946, he approached Dr Homai P. Dustoor of Bombay University to become the Head of the Department of English in the college and help in organizing the Honours course for English. Dr Dustoor was in a dilemma at this invitation as she was all set to go to Cambridge to do the English Tripos. But she was deeply impressed by Lala Shriram's sincerity and dedication to the cause of women's education. (An industrialist by profession, Lala Shriram invested a great deal of his wealth to promote education in several ways: by founding an educational trust, by endowing schools and colleges and by giving his unstinted attention to the institutions with which he was connected). She was eventually persuaded to defer her plans to go to Cambridge and join Indraprastha College.[36] Subsequently, she became the Principal of Lady Shri Ram College in Delhi. With a well equipped teaching staff, admissions to BA Honours and MA classes were made in 1946.

The students were jubilant at the introduction of these courses. Protima Mukerji, a student of the college in 1946, writes that with the introduction of Honours and MA classes, the college ceased to be a 'purely *purdah* college' since the students had to now go to the University for lectures in their Honours subject and MA classes. The beginning of these courses, Protima Mukerji says, broadened the life of the college, making it more interactive. It was easier now for the students to attend extra-curricular activities and lectures in the other colleges.[37] In fact, it was for the first time in 1946 that the students of Indraprastha College participated in an open competition in the University in inter-collegiate debates, elocution, and music competitions.

The year 1946 was significant for yet another decision regarding women students. Delhi University in this year abolished special prizes for women competitors participating in inter-college extra-curricular activities, thus establishing parity between men and women students and highlighting the fact that women were not a weaker sex who needed to be put in a special category. In these different ways, Delhi University in general and Indraprastha College in particular, continued to grow, diversify, and consolidate, encountering and conquering fresh challenges.

NOTES AND REFERENCES

1. Nirmala Sherjung, 'Sharing Some Experiences'.
2. Ibid.
3. Ibid.
4. Indu Vyas, 'Katto', *Pradeep*, November 1944.
5. Ibid.

6. Letter to the Editor from Delhi Provincial Students Federation, *The Hindustan Times*, 30 July, 1942.

7. Letter to the Editor from Lala Jagdish Prasad, Honorary Secretary of the governing body of Indraprastha College, *The Hindustan Times,* 7 August, 1942.

8. 'Educational Reform', *The Hindustan Times*, 17 June, 1940.

9. 'Delhi University To Be Reorganized: Central Government Accepts Vice Chancellor's Scheme: Proposed All India Cultural Centre', *The Hindustan Times*, 16 February, 1940.

10. Ibid.

11. Ibid.

12. 'Development of Delhi University: Object of Changes: Progress Described by Sir Maurice Gwyer', *The Statesman*, 13 May, 1942.

13. Aparna Basu, 'The Foundation And Early History Of Delhi University', in R.E. Frykenberg (ed.), *Delhi Through The Ages: Essays in Urban History, Culture and Society*, Oxford University Press, New Delhi, 1988, pp. 421, 423.

14. 'Development of Delhi University: Object of Changes: Progress Described by Sir Maurice Gwyer'.

15. Ibid.

16. Ibid.

17. Ibid.

18. Letter to the Editor by Lala Jagdish Prasad, Honorary Secretary of the governing body of Indraprastha College entitled 'Delhi University', *The Statesman*, 1 June, 1942.

19. Lala Jagdish Prasad to the Vice Chancellor, 30 April, 1942.

20. Ibid.

21. Letter to the Editor by Maurice Gwyer entitled 'Delhi University', *The Statesman*, 2 June, 1942.

22. S. Dutt (ed.), *The Delhi University Magazine*, Vol. 2, No. 1, April 1945, pp. 7–8.

23. S. Dutt (ed.), *The Delhi University Magazine*, Vol. 3, No. 1, April 1946, p. 10.

24. Aparna Basu, 'The Foundation and Early History of Delhi University', p. 423.

25. Sarup Singh, 'Reminiscences' in *Lala Shriram: Remembering Lala Shriram: Reminiscences on his 100th Birthday.*

26. Letter from Dr Ram Kishore, member of the governing body of Indraprastha College to Maurice Gwyer, 6 July, 1943.

27. Ibid.

28. Jagdish Prasad, Honorary Secretary to Lala Banwari Lal, Chairman, Governing Body, Indraprastha College, 12 July, 1943, in Revision of College Society Rules, 3 April, 1936 to 6 August, 1959.

29. Ibid.

30. Ibid.

31. Mr G. Goswami to Lala Shriram, Chairman, Governing Body, Indraprastha College, 3 January, 1959.

32. Memorandum regarding the appointment of a Principal, 29 August, 1943.

33. Ibid.

34. Ibid.

35. Sita Parmanand, 'Annual Report of Indraprastha College', in S. Dutt (ed.), *The Delhi University Magazine*, Vol. 3, No. 1, April 1946, p. 79.

36. Homai P. Dustoor, 'Reminiscences' in *Lala Shriram: Remembering Lala Shriram*.

37. Protima Mukerji, 'Looking Back'.

6

Azad Hindustan: Confident Strides of Women, 1947–59

The celebrations and festivities of Independence were marred by brutalities. Partition and communal violence destroyed lives and rendered families homeless. In the compulsive crossing of the borders, many were separated from their loved ones—family members, and friends.

TRAUMA OF PARTITION

Partition affected the lives of millions; women were the worst sufferers. Ritu Menon and Kamla Bhasin have argued that 1947 was 'a gendered narrative of displacement and dispossession ... of the realignment of family, community and national identities' in which the people were compelled to accommodate to 'the dramatically altered reality that now prevailed'.[1] Many women—and estimates range from 80,000 to 150,000—were raped and abducted during this time. Since women were seen as 'dependents of patriarchal households', both India and Pakistan devised 'special' regulations and procedures for their 'recovery and restoration'.[2] Of these large numbers of women, only 30,000 women were 'recovered' by 1957. The stories of these women were not the same. Some had faced terrifying brutalities and had agreed to be 'rescued' whereas several others had compromised with the new situation and resisted their 'recovery', which they considered a 'second abduction'. Not particularly sensitive to the sentiments of these women, the state had assumed the role of 'father-patriarch' to enforce the concept of legitimate families.[3] Feminist scholars, in the recent past, have questioned the irrationality and insensitivity of the state at that time towards women.

The trauma of Partition and communalism engulfed the city of Delhi, not sparing even the University and its students. It may be appropriate here to relate the experiences of Subhadra Butalia, a Russian language course student at the University of Delhi in 1946–47. Butalia, like many post-graduate women students in those days, lived in Miranda House hostel, which was a hostel for women before it became a second college for women in 1948.[4] Butalia remembers that 15 August 1947 was a Sunday and as was the custom, the girls had decided to go for an outing. Rajaram, the Principal of St. Stephen's College, usually escorted the girls and took them in his jeep. That day they decided to go to the Red Fort. There they saw four girls in a *tonga* (horse-driven cart), being threatened by a man with a knife. In a bid to protect themselves the girls jumped out of the *tonga* but the man gave chase. It is difficult to ascertain, writes Butalia, what happened to those girls. The entire area of Red Fort was strewn with bodies and blood. Principal Rajaram contacted the police station, only to be told that no police force was available and nothing could be done in the matter. Although Butalia and her friends could reach the hostel safely, all was not safe and peaceful in the University. It was, in fact, in the throes of loot and arson. The house of a renowned Professor of History, I.H. Qureshi, who was then teaching at St. Stephen's College, was ransacked. All his belongings, including valuable paintings, were looted. Fearing that their hostel could be attacked any moment, they rushed to protect Butalia's roommate, Zahira Hilali who was the niece of Sir Syed Ahmad Khan. Zahira was saved that day but the girls realized her life was in danger—killings and loot continued unabated in the University, and there was the possibility of Miranda hostel being attacked any time. One day, Subhadra Butalia recounts, a man rushed into the hostel and dragged out Zahira before the hostel students could react. The girls came to know later that the man was Zahira's brother, who had been informed of an impending mob attack on the hostel. As anticipated, a mob stormed the hostel, looking for Zahira. The mob's mood turned even uglier as they realized that Zahira had escaped. Fearing that in its frustration, the mob could become aggressive and violent towards the other girls, the warden of Miranda House hostel locked the girls in one room and subsequently shifted them to Principal Rajaram's house.[5]

A few sensitive young women of Indraprastha College responded to the situation in their own way, either organizing meetings in the college to urge the need for communal harmony or arranging debates on topical issues, with the objective of spreading peace and cordiality amongst different communities. To reach out to a wider group of students, they wrote articles published in the annual college magazine, *Pradeep*. S. Vaish in an article in the college magazine regretted the deeds of inhuman cruelty that had engulfed India in 1947 and 1948. She spoke of the 'bloody and ghastly tale of the past month', when men were 'hacked to pieces, women robbed of their honour and virtue and children dashed against the rocks.'[6] Homes and hearths were uprooted and family members separated from each other. It was ironical that Hindus and Muslims perpetrated such brutalities on each other when neither Hinduism nor Islam preaches the philosophy of hatred and intolerance nor do they teach deceit and suspicion. Moreover, Hindus and Muslims share several common bonds of traditions and customs. Citing the examples of Poland, Turkey, China, and Greece which were torn by power politics, Vaish urged the two communities to appreciate the strength of unity and reminded them that division had always engendered death and destruction in all parts of the world. She appealed to her fellow students 'to sink all petty differences and pool their energies and lend the strength of their enlightened minds for the achievement and maintenance of communal harmony.'[7]

The students of Indraprastha College also continued to be active as ever in public rallies and demonstrations. When Gandhi went on a fast to restore communal harmony, the students of the college, to show their support to Gandhi, took out a procession from the college to Gandhi Maidan and from there to Ramlila Grounds. They organized yet another procession to Azad Park. Sarla Sharma was arrested and imprisoned for five weeks in October 1947 for her involvement in such activities Sardar Patel was the home minister then and the Government of India in the few months after Independence followed a restrictive policy, enforcing detention without trial. It was in such circumstances that Sarla Sharma was imprisoned and kept in Delhi jail with criminal women. Why did the Government of India use tactics of coercion and denial of fundamental rights even upon such sensitive, rational Indian citizens who worked for peace and harmony in the society and relief for the refugees? It could be that the Government's severity was necessitated by the need to assert its control in the face of the extraordinary circumstances caused by the madness of communalism. Sarla Sharma was released on 17 November, 1947 after five weeks of detention in Delhi jail. No government pressures could transform her. She continued to work for communal harmony and relief of the refugees with undaunted spirit and enthusiasm.

GANDHI'S ASSASSINATION

The growing intolerance and the traumatic experiences of January 1948 indicate that the Government's repressive strategies had not succeeded at least against the mad assassins and the communalists. It could not even protect the life of the nation's messiah of peace and love. Gandhi succumbed to the irrational, violent, and brutal attack of Nathu Ram Godse on 30 January, 1948. The sense of despondency and despair pervading the nation was aggravated with Gandhi's assassination. Like most Indians throughout the nation, the students of Indraprastha College were shocked by Gandhi's death. Sharing Nehru's sentiments, they passed a resolution stating that 'The light has gone out of our lives and there is darkness everywhere'. We give an extract from the students' resolution:

Our beloved Bapu, the father of our nation was cruelly wrenched away from our midst by the violent hands of an assassin. But this foul deed, instead of plunging us into the horrors of a fratricidal strife, as it had really meant to, has really increased our faith in the Mahatma and his doctrine of non-violence and strengthened our hope in the ultimate triumph of good over evil.[8]

To share their grief with the larger community, the students attended an all-women condolence meeting in the memory of Gandhi at Purdahbagh.[9] The special prayers for Gandhi continued till the middle of February 1948. In their determined resolve to keep the spirit and values of Gandhi alive, the girls collected contributions for the Gandhi Memorial Fund. In mourning for Gandhi, Indraprastha College organized no entertainment on the College Day of 1948. It was a sombre, sober function to which Maulana Azad, the education minister, was invited to receive the guard of honour.

Motivated and inspired by the Gandhian philosophy and values, the girls of Indraprastha College engaged themselves in social welfare and community service. And, in 1948–49, no other service could have been more philanthropic than relief work for the refugees or helping them in stabilizing their lives. In aid of the refugees, the students organized a fancy *bazaar* in February 1948 and presented its net profit to the Prime Minister's Relief Fund. They also organized a fete in aid of the Prime Minister's Relief Fund, to support refugee students. To urge the Prime Minister that the fete collections should be earmarked only for refugee students, the girls personally visited Nehru to hand over the money. That day happened to be *Holi*. Nehru was surprised that the girls had abstained from playing *Holi*. Reportedly, when Nehru inquired the reason for not playing *Holi*, they burst into tears. Moved by their grief Nehru asked: 'Is it because of Gandhiji?' Appreciating the emotions of the students, he said 'we mourn him but you must carry on the work Bapu left for us to finish.'[10] *Holi* was not celebrated in 1948. It had come too soon after Gandhi's assassination.

The refugee problem and the assassination of Gandhi overcast the years 1947–49. But a matter of equally grave concern was facilitating education for women from West Punjab. It was mentioned earlier that Indraprastha College along with Hindu and Ramjas colleges had started classes in the second shift in 1947. Following the government instructions, these classes were continued till 1949. Indraprastha College, as the only women's college in Delhi till 1948, admitted all such women from West Punjab who were keen on pursuing subjects in humanities and social sciences. But as more and more women sought education, there was the problem of overflowing numbers. Several girls were compelled to take admission in co-educational colleges like Hindu and St. Stephen's. Unlike the present times, these colleges were not at all popular amongst the girls and, more significantly, with their families. The sex ratio of the students in St. Stephen's College in 1947–49 was roughly 6 girls to 400 boys. Of these girls, some were not allowed to attend classes by their families.[11] The custom of *purdah* was still alive. In such circumstances, there was a desperate need for another women's college and Miranda House was the answer. Miranda House was established as a college in March 1948.

Till 1956, two women's colleges—Indraprastha College and Miranda House—stood solidly to fulfil the increasing needs of women's education. With the growing demand for higher education for women, Lala Shriram once again came to the forefront. An industrialist by profession but an educationist to the core, he laid the foundation of yet another all-women institution, Lady Shri Ram College, in 1956, in memory of his wife. Shri Ram College of Commerce was also established by him as early as 1926. (Lala Shri Ram was also associated with Indraprastha College in its pioneering years. He continued to be on the governing bodies of Indraprastha, Hindu and Ramjas colleges and Lady Shri Ram College and Shri Ram College of Commerce, of which he was the founder member.)

INDRAPRASTHA COLLEGE MOVES ON

In 1950, Indraprastha College celebrated its silver jubilee. The first 25 years of the college show the making of strong, confident, socially responsible women who fought the *purdah* system, broke the norms of patriarchy, and seldom hesitated to be in the midst of politics and national events. This truly cosmopolitan institution showed spontaneous growth over 25 years, from a humble beginning to a centre of knowledge and culture. From a measly 7 students in 1924 the number of students admitted to college had shown a remarkable increase to 610 in 1950. This rapid increase in the number of students was accompanied by a corresponding expansion in the staff, that is, from one teacher in 1924 to 29 in 1950. The college showed significant progress not only in its size but also in its results. Compared to the other colleges of Delhi University, Indraprastha College showed the highest pass percentage between 1940 and 1950.

We have illustrated through various examples that since its inception, the students of the college had played an important social role, were actively engaged in national politics, and had demonstrated tremendous organizing abilities. Here, we would highlight the academic achievements and professional distinctions they had earned till 1950. The list of achievers is endless. We are citing only a few for the sake of illustration. Rasil Manohar Singh, apart from being a student of the college, had also served on the teaching staff of the college for a few years. Subsequently, she obtained a fellowship to Law School at Yale, USA and obtained the LL.M. degree from the same University in 1948. She then obtained an internship in the UNO for six weeks and later served on the secretariat staff of the Human Rights Division of UNO. While at UNO, she was awarded a scholarship to attend a course of lectures on International Law at the Hague. Another student, Sarla Bhargava, obtained an internship in the UNO in 1949. Lotika

Sarkar, after her post-graduation went to Cambridge to study for a doctor's degree in Law. She was later appointed the Director of Studies in Law at Newnham College, Cambridge.

Recognizing the achievements of its students, the college also encouraged its teachers to develop and enhance their academic qualifications. It devised a system of granting study leave to such teachers who wished to pursue higher studies. C.K. Kausukutty, head of the Department of Economics and, Mardhekar, head of the Department of English were granted study leave to pursue doctoral programmes in their respective subjects. Kausukutty joined the London School of Economics and Mardhekar joined King's College, London. Apart from teachers who left for other shores to pursue their education, there were teachers like Indumati Datar from the Department of Sanskrit who earned their Ph.D. degree from Bombay University.

The college encouraged the students to not only enhance their academic excellence but, emphasizing the overall development of the personality, it also stressed the importance of extra-curricular abilities such as debating, drama, oratory, creative writing talents, and social work. The debating and the literary societies of the Students' Union reflect the students' political consciousness, their mature understanding of the contemporary events, and their sensitivity to social issues.

The unusual grit and determination of the students of the college was demonstrated over the issue of the construction of the swimming pool. When the students demanded a swimming pool in the 1950s, the initial response of the college authorities was negative. They could not construct it for the lack of finances. But this did not weaken the enthusiasm of the students. They volunteered to perform *shramdan*. The earnestness of the girls and the financial support from the UGC and the college authorities made the swimming pool a possibility in 1956. The UGC agreed to provide the major part of the necessary funds if the college staff and the students could provide labour. The swimming pool was completed by November 1957 and inaugurated in the same month by Professor V.K.R.V. Rao, the vice chancellor of Delhi University.[12] Indraprastha College thus became the first women's college in Delhi to have its own swimming pool and till today, it is the only women's college in Delhi University to have such a facility.

By 1960, the college students were showing a growing interest in a number of sports. As an incentive, the college introduced the system of 'college colours'. This was another first: the college became the first women's college in Delhi to confer such an honour on athletes and players who had shown outstanding and extraordinary performance during the year.

The college pioneered the Tutor-Ward system in 1960—a system that is now followed in almost all the colleges of Delhi University. The purpose was to initiate and orient the first year students who might feel strange after a well-protected school life. The tutors were required to develop and encourage the interests and the hidden skills of their wards by organizing academic discussions or cultural and sports events. It was often through the Tutor-Ward system that the talents of the students were identified and channelled into the different activities of the college.

By the 1960s, a string of women's colleges had appeared in Delhi but these in no way dwarfed Indraprastha College. It stood strong and distinguished as a pioneer in women's education. Its early inception had given it a headstart that it strove to maintain. The college over the years acquired a distinct character, maintaining its liberal hue, and absorbing modern and radical ideas. The students continue to be involved in a plethora of activities—from academic and cultural programme to collection drives for the Prime Minister's relief fund. The elitist beginnings of the college had made its earlier students seek subjects like history and philosophy but the horizons widened in later years to include subjects like economics, mathematics, and psychology; in the 1970s commerce was introduced and in the 1980s and 1990s, vocational subjects. By 1960s, the college had evolved from the days when its students were mostly daughters of 'brown sahibs' from the princely states and the top echelons of the Indian society, acquiring a multi-faceted identity, and catering to the wider sections of the country. There were also students from Africa and Southeast Asia seeking educational avenues here.

As Delhi continued to expand and with it, women's colleges, Indraprastha College once again generated a quiet revolution championed by its former students and faculty members. Many of them began to teach in the newly established colleges. Several of them became Principals of these colleges. To name a few—C.K. Kausukutty became the Principal of Lakshmibai College; Saraswati Rao of Jankidevi Mahavidyalaya; Homai Dustoor of Lady Shri Ram College; Indira Thakurdas of Gargi College; Sita Nambiar of Daulat Ram College; Krishna Gorowara of Kamla Nehru College; and Sheila Uttamsingh of Indraprastha College. Thus, despite the flurry of colleges, Indraprastha College remained the fountainhead of women's education in Delhi.

Notes and References

1. Ritu Menon and Kamla Bhasin, 'Recovery, Rupture; Resistance: Indian State and Abduction of Women During Partition', *Economic and Political Weekly*, Vol. 28 No. 17, April 1993, p. WS2.

2. Ibid., pp. WS3–WS4.

3. Ibid., pp. WS2–WS11.

4. Miranda House, an all-women's college, was a dream of Maurice Gwyer, a dream he had hoped to fulfil in 1947. However, the college could only be established a year later in 1948. The vice chancellor, it is reported, had a small, framed watercolor sketch of the college in his office. It was with much affection and warmth that he had spoken of the transformation of the hostel into a college. See Rati Bartholomew, 'Early Days at Miranda, 1947–49' in Uma Chakravarty, Radhika Singha, Ramya Sreenivasan (ed.), *Reliving Miranda, 1948–98*, p. 14.

5. Subhadra Butalia, 'Miranda before Miranda: Fragments of a Past', in ibid., pp. 20–21.

6. S. Vaish, 'Hindus and Muslims: Friends or Foes', *Pradeep*, May 1948.

7. Ibid.

8. 'The Editorial', *Pradeep*, May 1948.

9. Purdahbagh was near Indraprastha School, behind Jama Masjid. Women could organize assemblies and meetings here and young girls could play in the shelter of *purdah*.

10. Annual Report, Indraprastha College for Women, Golden Jubilee, 1924–74.

11. Rati Bartholomew, 'Early Days at Miranda, 1947–49', p. 14.

12. Sundari Siddharta, 'They Came to Jeer but Stayed On to Dig', *Golden Oriole, 1924–74* and Saroj Mathur, 'Swimming Pool Ban Gaya', *Pradeep*, November 1956.

Epilogue

'To look down upon miles of country, to see the roads and railways running through the fields, to see whole towns at once, to fly from summer conditions to winter conditions—these are things we would all like to experience in a glider. It is really wonderful to glide amongst the wandering clouds in calm and cool weather away from the mundane world.' These words were written by Raj Mitroo, a student of Indraprastha College, in an article titled 'How I Learnt Gliding' for the 1961 issue of the college magazine *Pradeep*. She had been flying since 1958 and in 1961 had established a record for solo flying in a glider. The lines above could well be taken as a metaphor for the ethos and mood of the nation and its women and as a microcosm of both these, the world of the students of Indraprastha College in the late 1950s and early 60s.

Raj Mitroo's passion for gliding represents the motivation and drive of a small section of Indian women—their urge to break barriers and strive for positive achievements. A small number of middle-class women were quietly concentrating on consolidating exploring opportunities and skills. They were making forays into male bastions. One fervent ambition was to enter the Civil Services.

Teaching, medicine, and nursing were careers which the miniscule number of college-educated women in the 1930s and 40s could aspire for. After Independence Indian women could stretch their ambitions towards the civil services. Having made a headstart so far as college education in northwest India is concerned, Indraprastha College has had a fair number of alumni in the two premier services, the IAS and

IFS. However in the 1960s Indian society was still traditional in its attitude towards leadership roles for women. The rules that guided the marriage or postings of women civil servants reveal the prejudices of a deeply conservative society and the male bias of the services. Very few and extremely outstanding women were able to enter the civil services at first, and desirable postings and promotions were often not easy.

Metropolitan Indian middle classes in the early 1960s were largely persuaded that sending their daughters to colleges for one or two years was necessary. However, they were not equally convinced about the motive for college education. Very few women would have either desired or were destined for a career. It might be instructive to consider the fortunes of a group of 13 girls who entered Indraprastha College in 1959 to study English Literature. Three of them went on to do their post-graduation and became college teachers. Two taught in schools. One works as a parliamentary interpreter. The one who secured a first division in BA married immediately after. Marriage was also on the cards for two others who hailed from prosperous business families. For the rest of the class of 1959 there is no information, but it is unlikely that they adopted any professions. This kind of a situation would have been typical for the early 60s.

The surface of life at the University, especially for its women students, was placid and this was true at Indraprastha as well. In fact, the period immediately following India's independence was a passive one for Indian women. There could be an explanation for the compliant ethos of the 1950s for Indian women. It appears that after the tumultuous involvement in national politics activated by Gandhian strategies, the mass of women in India were content to sink back into domestic bliss. Perhaps there was a prevailing feeling that with the nation on its way towards progress and the family sphere rendered safe, women should return to non-aggressive modes of life. Emphasizing the mood of cooperation between the citizenry and the government up to the mid-1960s, Nivedita Menon argues that 'the women's movement, by and large, settled down to co-operate with the government in development programmes and gradual institutionalization. In addition, the characterization of the post-independence state as an ally in progressive transformation, economic and social, was an inevitable hangover from the independence struggle.'[1]

To a certain extent this kind of retreat was inherent in the Gandhian methodology of struggle by women. Contemporary historians are persuaded that Gandhi's conception of women's political activity did not envisage their abandonment of traditional roles. Neerja Choudhury points this out as she tries to determine the causes of the under-representation of responsible political activity or position of Indian women in the early post-Independence years. 'While women participated in large numbers in the national movement, and it improved their status within the existing framework of family and society, it did not create a significant change in the lives of the women outside. Nor did it lead to a debate to question the social mores which gave primacy to wifehood or motherhood.'[2] In Choudhury's opinion the Gandhian methods of political activity for women did not prepare them for the post-1947 phase and the competitive model of politics, which encouraged the formation of sectional pressure groups.

In the post-Independence years, one of the few women who received some measure of success and recognition in the political sphere was Sucheta Kripalani, whose highest position was as the Governor of Uttar Pradesh. Kripalani was a student of Indraprastha College during the 1940s. Mukul Banerjee, Ambika Soni, Meira Kumar, Shama Singh are some other names of former students of Indraprastha who have adopted politics as their work, and have adhered to Congress politics for the majority of their career. All these women hail from the period of 1960 to 1970 in the College. Sarla Sharma, who appears in this narrative several times, is a political activist and a Communist Party worker since the 1940s. She has enjoyed many stints as Municipal Corporator of Delhi.

From 1966 there were signs that the spirit of the 60s was beginning to change. In fact, the late 60s and early 70s were periods of unprecedented assertion of youth discontent and power. Governments all over the world had a tough task contending with the youth movements fuelled by different ideologies and ideals. That the tremors of these changes were reflected in the calm waters of Indraprastha College is evident in the articles written by the students in the college magazine, *Pradeep*. Meera Joshi, a student in 1967, wrote an article on 'Trend in Modern Youth: Hippism'. She was referring to a large group of disaffected western youth who rejected the competitive materialistic culture of the West and whose rebellion consisted not of political protests but embracing Eastern religious cults and intake of drugs. Joshi criticized them as being a 'leaderless movement'. Another article by an anonymous contributor, who had visited the Haight-Ashbury district in New York, has the comment: 'The hippies seemed to me to be young adolescents who wanted to be children and regretted the adulthood that faces them.' Perhaps this reaction betokens pragmatism in the Indian student who in the 60's did not find material affluence so plentiful in her country to be able to express rejection or disgust of it.

The tumult in the young adult world overseas was attracting the attention of Indians. Renee Boruah, another student of Indraprastha College, betrays admiration for the western protest movements in her article 'Is Youth Powerful? In the US and India'. Chitra Muliyil's thoughtful article questions the aim of education. She questioned 'What Are We Being Educated For? The education we receive at the moment helps none to answer any questions, except the examination paper. The BA course should not be sold so cheaply. The Honours course should be scrapped, and everyone should receive a more balanced education.'

It would be incorrect to assume that changes in Indian youth and Indian society at this time were ignited solely by inspiration from the West. The second phase and the most ideologically fervent phase of the youth movement in India looked up to the charismatic leader of the East, Chairman Mao Tse Tung. Tilottama Sharma observes, 'Caught between the turbulent currents of the East and West, the Indian campuses also experienced a wave of student insurgency in the 1960s. Though the nature of the movement, its course and extent were qualitatively different from both the New Left Movement and the Chinese 'Red Guard' Movement, yet some of the basic issues involved in it were strikingly similar to both these movements.'[3] Sharma avers that the radical Indian students rejected the parliamentary line taken by the Indian communists, as well as the Soviet model. 'They considered Maoism a more suitable model for the Indian revolution.'[4]

The impact of Maoism on the students of Delhi University resulted in the formation of two groups consisting of the leftist students of the campus, Yugantak and Sankalp. Yugantak was an association of a small group of Maoist students, who formed an organization named Student-Youth Federation (SYF), with the aim of carrying forward the cause of an armed struggle of workers and peasants guided by Marxism-Leninism-Mao Zedong thought. The members of SYF expressed solidarity with the masses through meetings with the workers in the working-class areas of the city. Within the campus they challenged the prevailing system of education. There were heated debates with leading intellectuals in the University regarding courses of study, economics, or political systems in India. The SYF also organized protest demonstrations against American intervention in Vietnam.

The SYF was also influenced by the ideas of the Naxalite Revolution, which had fired their colleagues in Calcutta. At a meeting held in 1969, it was decided that the SYF members should start moving into the rural areas where Naxalite activities were already on. Thus, inspired by revolutionary zeal, a group of students and young teachers of the University gave up their careers and jobs in order to integrate with the masses.

Urvashi Butalia, co-founder of the feminist publishing house, Kali for Women (now the owner of Zubaan), was a student of Miranda House in those years. She reminisces: 'Our years at the University were marked by profound political developments around us. Suddenly we heard of our contemporaries going underground. They were going off to Naxalbari. Things were happening in the colleges.'[5] Akila Sivadas, of Miranda House, describes the heady feelings, the widening of mental horizons that young people experienced: 'We found to our great excitement that our existence was not so mundane. In fact our destiny was not a problem, not because we had got everything worked out, but because we were too busy deciding the destiny of the nation.'[6]

No written records are available to tell us what was taking place in Indraprastha College in this period. One has to construct life in the college in Naxalite times from verbal reminiscences. Away from the tense excitement of the campus, leftist political activities had created ripples here. A small unit of the Progressive Students Union flourished in the college. Within the precincts of the college there was not so much action as discussion. One is informed that the otherwise stern and disciplinarian Principal Bina Dasgupta allowed the lawns in front of the college to be used for meetings of the discussion groups.

The tide of student activism was noticeable in other spheres as well. Among the politically conscious students of Indraprastha College, there was a strong feeling of solidarity with the North Vietnamese people who were opposing the South Vietnamese backed by USA. Sumi Krishna, a student then, captures the commotion and commitment of those times, in an article in the college magazine of 1970, titled 'Of Ice-creams and Henry VIII': 'Of processions, of marching silently for Gandhi and peace through the university and noisily to the USIS, shouting *Amar Nam Tumar Nam, Vietnam, Vietnam* and *Remember Dien-Bien-Phu.*'

The spirit of defiance amongst the students flourished not only in matters of international politics. Within the day-to-day life of the college they found much that dissatisfied them. A visible and highly colourful signs of the awakened consciousness of Indraprastha students were the slogans that appeared nightly on the walls of the college. They were freshly painted every time the authorities painted them over. One particular slogan from those times that has become famous in Indraprastha College lore is 'Women are not *roti* making machines'. From a letter of the Principal to the governing body we have an inkling of how helpless the college authorities felt in contending with the critical mood of the students. With regard to a proposal to increase hostel charges, the Principal confessed her inability to suggest the increase in fees, in view of the 'tense situation in the student world' saying 'students will not accept the increase'. The student movement of the 70s had changed the equation between the authorities and the youth.

An article in *The Indian Express* of 31 March, 1970, titled 'Growing Demands for Change', brings out clearly the change that had come over Indraprastha College in the late 60s and 70s. The article began by charging that earlier the college had presented 'an image of insularity to the outside world, it is because of the numerous do's and don'ts that regulated the lives of the students'. But in 1970 'the demand for change has reached an explosive quality. The IP college girl in whom rebelliousness was completely absent has become searching in her questions to the authorities. She wants Explanations.'

The activism and political participation of the women students and teachers was again evident in their reactions to the emergency imposed by Indira Gandhi in 1977. It was realized that the rights of civilians in a democracy needed constant vigilance so that they may never be infringed upon again. Conscientious citizens, academics, journalists, students, and lawyers strove to set in place an organization which could maintain a watch over instances of misuse of authority. The first Civil Rights Protective group that was formed was the People's Union of Civil Liberties and Democratic Rights. The venue for one of the many meetings held to discuss and formulate the exact nature of the Union's work, was Indraprastha College. The reason was that some teachers of the college were actively engaged in the Union.

Eventually there emerged two different civil liberties organizations. Some members of the original PUCLDR felt that civil liberties could not construe social reform alone. It had to support grass-root movements in the country. They formed an organization called the People's Union of Democratic Rights. The members of this organization, amongst whom there were some students and teachers of Indraprastha College, launched an intensive letter-writing campaign to reach out to the grass-root movements in remote parts of the country. They did not hesitate to venture out to distant, interior parts of the country to investigate instances of exploitation and injustice. In this work they avoided official hospitality and subsisted entirely on voluntary assistance. Apart from Indraprastha students, students from Miranda, Hindu and Ramjas Colleges also worked as PUDR activists.

During 1977–78, an organization that was active in the work of grass-root mobilization was Action India. Some teachers and students from Indraprastha were members of this group. The group conducted adult literacy programmes in resettlement colonies of Delhi such as Nand Nagiri and Jehangirpuri.

The national and international events throughout the 60s and 70s, resulted in widespread changes in the mental make-up of college-going women in India. The Vietnam War, the Civil Rights Movement in USA, the rise of Feminism, the left-oriented uprisings in Europe – all these could not fail to have an impact on students and teachers in Indian Universities. In India, the Naxalite Revolution in the 1970s, followed by the declaration of a state of Emergency by Indira Gandhi which brought into being the first democratic rights movement, had a profound effect on the changing mindscape of educated young people. By the end of the 1970s considerable political maturity had entered the consciousness of women in Indian colleges.

Indraprastha College completed 50 years of its existence in 1974 and celebrated its Golden Jubilee. This was also the year in which 'Towards Equality', a report on the status of women in India, was published. This was a momentous event as far as awareness about the reality of Indian women's lives was concerned. The United Nations had declared the decades between 1975 and 1985 as the International Women's Decade. Planning for these dedications began in 1971. The United Nations requested member nations to prepare status reports on the lives of women. In 1971, the Government of Indira Gandhi asked some women members of Parliament to prepare this report. The terms of reference were wide, ranging from examining constitutional provisions and gender discriminations in employment to suggesting legal and political reform. Much to the embarrassment of the Government, when the findings were published in 1974, in 'Towards Equality', it proved that 27 years after Independence, the status of women in India had worsened. For the first time, many hidden iniquities surfaced, as for instance, the falling sex ratio. Geraldine Forbes minced no words in characterizing 'Towards Equality' as the 'wake up call'.[7]

At the Government level, the revelation that 27 years of the development process had only increased the miseries of women in India impelled a spate of action. A Department of Social Welfare was set up at the centre. Under the ministry of Human Resource Development, a Department of Women and Child Development came into being. This particular government department initiated a scheme for basing women's development centres in certain selected colleges. Indraprastha College was one of the institutions selected under this scheme.

In 1974 there was a growing realization that women must carve out their areas of freedom. After the publication of 'Towards Equality', activist and critical scrutiny was focused on religious, cultural, political, and social mores. A spirit of combativeness manifested itself in tackling oppressive social customs such as dowry, *sati,* and issues of violence like rape and dowry deaths. The women's movement had a vigorous presence in Indraprastha College. The lively stirrings in the college attracted the media in 1979. Preeti Mehra, a journalist with *The Hindustan Times,* wrote in the article 'IP Not Quite Conservative': 'The College is in the transitional stage, progressing towards its ideal. What is important to note is that like most colleges it is not stagnant, most of its students aware of its shortcomings are striving and working towards a better Indraprastha.'[8] This newspaper article was occasioned by a protest rally organized under the initiative of Indraprastha College students against the harassment of women in Delhi Transport Corporation (DTC) buses. Commending the students, Preeti Mehra had written, 'Although independent of the Delhi University Students

Union, it has played its role in University rallies and protests against the Shah of Iran, the Chopra children's murder case, the dowry murders and headed the most recent, against eve-teasing in DTC buses.'[9] The agitation against the DTC began in 1979, when first a student and then a teacher were assaulted on a DTC bus. On 23 February 1979, the members of the Progressive Students Union in the College mobilized the men and women of the University to march to the Head Office of the Delhi Transport Corporation.

The militancy of the Indraprastha girls was once again visible when they initiated the first ever march-cum-demonstration against dowry murders. On hearing of a dowry death in the vicinity of the college, the Indraprastha College Women's Committee alerted Stri Sangharsh, an umbrella organization for several women's groups and organized a demonstration. Radha Kumar writes: 'Impetus for this demonstration came, in fact, from Indraprastha College Women's Committee, formed in 1978, who told Stri Sangharsh of the murder and suggested they demonstrate. The Indraprastha College Committee and the Progressive Student's Union all marched under the banner of *Stri Sangharsh*, adding both numbers and militancy.'[10] The impact of this first united action against dowry was far-reaching. Manini Das observes that this case became a catalyst for bringing together individual activists and women from different political and civil liberties groups around a common platform under the name of *Stri Sangharsh*.[11]

Another issue that galvanized women's groups in 1979 was the victimization of women from small non-metropolitan centres. The cases of Mathura Devi of Baghpat and Rameeza Bee of Hyderabad, poor and illiterate women who had been assaulted in police stations were infamous. The Indraprastha College Women's Committee along with the PUCLDR cooperated with some eminent lawyers in reopening investigations in these cases where gross injustice had been done.

Yet another issue that jolted all educated women in Delhi, activists and academics alike, was the revival of the custom of *sati* in north India in 1987. In 1987, in Deorala village in Rajasthan, Roop Kanwar, an 18-year-old bride, immolated herself on her husband's pyre. Fifteen women organizations set up a Joint Action Forum against *sati*. The Women's Development Centre of Indraprastha College also organized a *sati-virodhi* march, which was joined by several students from the colleges and schools of Delhi.

Women activists could not expect literacy amongst their target audience and therefore could not hope to reach out to women and men as widely as possible and sensitize them to deep-seated prejudices through writing. There was thus a need to develop visual literacy. Amrita Chachchi in her article 'Media as a Political Statement' remarked: 'If we take as alternative forms that are non-institutional then the women's movement in India reveals a tremendous creativity in the use of street theatre, exhibitions, posters and new kinds of leaflets in all its campaigns.'[12] Activist groups working in the field of women's welfare and trade unionists seized the medium of street theatre for creating awareness about contemporary social issues. These performances could be carried into the hearts of localities, villages, and bus stops, although college campuses were often the natural venues for these performances. Street theatre is an invaluable aid in disseminating consciousness regarding specific issues among the masses. Interactive element and teamwork are characteristics also present in another theatre movement of the time, theatre workshops. In Indraprastha College, beginning in 1968, throughout the 70s, Rati Bartholomew, a lecturer in the Department of English of the College, conducted theatre workshops with students of the college. Students from other colleges also participated in these workshops. The Indraprastha students, who were members of the Progressive Students Union and Action India, worked with the children living in the slum areas of Yamuna Pushta, Nandgiri, and Jehangirpuri. Dowry murders, widow burning, harassment and molestation of women, AIDS, plague, child rape—various evils, which afflict society and women in particular—were explored dramatically through the medium of street theatre.

These feminist activities can be linked to the cogitations in the Seminar on 'Women and Culture', organized by the Staff Association of Indraprastha College in April 1981. In their introductory presentation titled 'Reflection on Women and Culture', Kumkum Sangari and Sudesh Vaid of the English Department of the College argued that 'there is a growing awareness that the nature of the oppression of women is sited both in material conditions as well as in social and cultural attitudes and practices and so needs to be combated at both levels.'[13] The seminar singled out areas of analysis such as Sanskrit texts, the epics, Buddhist literature, Meerabai the poet-saint, erotic love poetry, classical dance, contemporary journals, cinema and Indo-Anglian literature, as well as socio-religious and political movements. Four years later, when Sangari and Vaid reflected on the seminar, they found that this project on women studies was too broad, too ambitious and that many links had not been established. Yet in 1981, the seminar on 'Women and Culture', stirred discussion on contentious traditions.

In fact, the years beginning in the late 1970s revived the flavour of the 1940s Quit India Movement in Indraprastha College. The same fervour in participating in stirring marches and demonstrations was witnessed. Principal Dr Sheila Uttamsingh's speech in 1974, during the Golden Jubilee celebrations, stressed that in Indraprastha College, 'history runs parallel with the history of our struggle for independence. It mirrors the many cultural, social and economic changes that have been witnessed in the last fifty years.' This speech also referred to the expressed feeling of students that 'we cling to traditional values but we are not dwellers in an ivory tower'.

In the 1990s the economic system in the country reversed its direction. The nation shook itself off from the earlier planned socialist economy to the market-oriented, liberalized system in line with prevailing trend worldwide. Market directed concerns have affected all spheres of life. Higher education has not escaped the consequences of the changing conditions of the economy.

The obligation to provide an education that would ultimately provide a livelihood was bringing about an expansion of the curriculum in different disciplines. Commerce and accountancy, information technology and business management became dominant fields. Skills relevant to these subjects were in demand in the rapidly burgeoning corporate world. Commerce was introduced as a subject of study at the BA Honours level in Indraprastha College in 1977. According to a survey article in the newsmagazine *India Today* of 21 June, 2001, Indraprastha College figures among the top five colleges in Delhi teaching commerce.

The University, colleges, the UGC, students—all were convinced by the middle of the 1990s that in the surcharged atmosphere induced by liberalization, professional skills had to be imparted to young people. It was not possible for the University or its constituent colleges to withstand the forces that were shaping the country and the world. Computer application, a discipline that was acquiring immense importance, was introduced in Indraprastha College first as a subject in the BA Pass Course. Subsequently, initiating the first of its self-financing schemes, the college introduced the Bachelor of Computer Application Course. It was the first women's college in the north campus of Delhi University to introduce this course. The aim was to impart training in computer applications in a serious and integrated system. It was designed to be different from the perfunctory and commercial fashion in which this skill was taught in the market place.

In continuation of its efforts to provide market-and job-oriented programmes in the colleges, the UGC appointed a committee chaired by eminent educationist Abid Hussain to inquire into the viability of introducing such programmes in the colleges. It was also to investigate ways of integrating these courses into the existing system. The committee recommended six degree courses and one post-graduate diploma in Global Trade Management. The six bachelor degree courses were to be in Mass Media and Mass Communication, Financial Analysis, Bio-medical Sciences, Nutrition and Health Education, Tourism and Travel Management, and Biotechnology. Indraprastha College introduced the degree course in Mass Media and Mass Communication in 1999. This was the first mass media and mass communication course for undergraduates in Delhi. The increasing demand for media courses and its proliferation in the education system point to the importance this field has come to occupy in the competitive world of employment in India.

As privatization and commercialization of education progressed relentlessly, the educators could ignore the hard realities of the changing situation at their peril. But for the young ones there was no dilemma, there were no options. For them there was only the law of survival in the forest of capitalism. The government pleaded resource crunch and encouraged institutions imparting professional training such as the IITs, to become self-supporting by raising funds through interactions with industry. Universities were also urged to examine ways of raising finances to offset the cost of running institutions. The Rastogi Committee was appointed in 1997 to make a set of recommendations to take into account the changed scenario.

Several members of the teaching community raised their voice in dissent against the market-oriented changing trends in higher education. In 1997, the Forum for Democratic Struggle of the Delhi University Teachers for Academic Reform took up cudgels to resist these developments in a pamphlet titled, 'The Crisis in Higher Education: the Rastogi Committee and the Tasks Ahead for the Teachers Movement'. The pamphlet held market forces, responsible for changing the orientation of higher education. It argued that the recommendations of the Rastogi Committee were pointed towards the total subservience of higher education to industry, agriculture, trade, and commerce and charged that the committee's understanding of 'social' needs was in the context of liberalization and the needs of imperialism and landlordism.

There was a sequel to these discussions. In 1999–2000, the teaching community was agitated by a set of proposals made by some Indian industrialists. The name of Mukesh Ambani of the Reliance Industries figured prominently in these. Seeking to alleviate the high cost of technical education and the sciences, these corporates were willing to finance university education in certain disciplines. The focus of these proposals was that corporate houses were willing to step into the field of higher education, especially in technology and applied sciences. This, it was felt, would reduce the resource crunch. In other words, the business houses would finance higher education of a certain kind, or more appropriately a few, chosen fields, from which they hoped to reap benefits in terms of trained personnel and research findings in future.

The apprehension of teachers was that colleges and universities might allow certain scholarly disciplines to die out because of lack of corporate encouragement and unviability in the job market. The fear was that eventually only those subjects would remain which have a demand in the market-oriented society of the times.

To inquire into the situation in higher education in the context of changing economic realities, Indraprastha College as a part of its Platinum Jubilee celebrations, organized a National Seminar on 'Humanities and Social Sciences in Higher Education Policy: Challenges and Responses' in April 1999. The seminar gathered together thinkers from the world of technical and professional education, as well as humanities and social sciences. The emphasis was on finding ways out of the stalemate.

Contentious positions were presented and a wide variety of solutions offered. Pramod Talgeri of CIEFL, Hyderabad, vigorously protested that 'the University cannot be handled like a profit making factory of a private limited company with the vice chancellor as its managing director trying to raise funds. The University will and should remain the responsibility of the state in the interests of the state.' Kapil Kapoor of Jawaharlal Nehru University gave an equally strong and categorical direction for change: 'to make this education meaningful and intellectually fruitful and to make it serve its purpose we have to turn it towards the villages and the poor and make it village envisioned and relocate it in the attested Indian cultural and intellectual traditions of learning and thought'. Anil Sadgopal of Central Institute of Education, Delhi, stressed the 'transformative rather than status-quoist role of higher education' and insisted upon 'educational institutions as social processes with a role in generating knowledge for social development of a specified region'.

Two pragmatic professionals, V. Raju, Director, IIT Delhi, and M. Athreya, management consultant, represented the opposite poles from the speakers mentioned above. Raju prescribed fruitful collaboration between higher education and industry, which had been successfully implemented in IIT. Athreya conceded that the shift from social to technical courses was inevitable in the 'early stages of structural change'. He posited a kind of interdependency between techno-managerial and humanities courses, stipulating that human sensitivity and social conscience are needed by those working in the economic sphere. He further argued that 'even those working in government, NGOs and civil society, will need, in addition to their social science knowledge-base some core skills'.

Reconciliation between streams of courses was, however, advised by Sumi Krishna, an environmentalist and IP alumnus. She deplored the 'iron-frame' and argued that 'subject combinations which seem quite rational and socially relevant in the students own perceptions are dismissed by the guardians of higher education. What is required is to loosen the rigid framework so that students can step across disciplines, choosing courses rather than subjects.' Meena Bhargava, too, advocated the loosening of the rigid framework of higher education. Opposing privatization of education or industry-oriented education, she pointed towards 'integrated courses to bring the balance between science and social science' and observed that due to the 'adherence to strict teacher-student ratio, we are not able to offer additional courses which may be of wider interest or employ specialists from different fields'. Nandita Narain, a mathematician from St. Stephen's College, in common with the latter two panelists, devoted her presentation to devising new schemes for rejuvenating the teaching of social sciences.

In this medley of voices, of vigorous debate between teachers opposed to commercialization of higher education and the government, what were student voices articulating? The whole debate concerned them—their minds, careers, personalities. If we accept articles in student magazines as the medium of their expression, we might glance at a few issues of the Indraprastha College magazine, *Aaroh*. In the 1990–91 issue of the magazine, there is an ironical poem by Harvinder Kaur on the difficulties of launching a career in journalism without adequate training. She was a student of English Literature and had ventured courageously into freelance journalism. Subsequently she returned to the University for an MA degree. In her words,

Before you consider 'to be or not to be'
You're back, trudging for an MA degree
Even freelancing is not too free
Papa can't waste money
On a type-writer and camera. You see

In the 1994–95 issue of *Aaroh*, an article titled 'AISEC – A Movement Striving Towards Excellence' by Divya Kashyap of Economics Honours argues that as far as the students are concerned there are no doubts in their minds regarding interaction with the corporate world. Among the four objectives of AISEC outlined by the author the second and third were, 'to bridge the gap between the student world and the corporate sector' and 'to inculcate managerial skills amongst its members through practical experience'.

However, not all young minds were equally enthusiastic about the pre-eminence of the corporate world. In an article 'Liberalization vs. Globalization', published in *Aaroh* 1996, Purnima Singh, a student of Political Science Honours, wrote that 'the fundamentals of the Indian situation conflict with the basic ideals of globalization'. In her opinion, liberalization 'has no answer for those who fall outside the global market and therefore it has no answer for the foremost of India's problems—hunger, poverty and unemployment'. Yet in conclusion she admitted to the inevitability of liberalization. She observed, 'no matter whether to the East or to the West, one comes across only different versions of the same point of view—economic liberalization is the only route through which prosperity can come'.

In this onslaught of a market-driven economy and society, the liberal arts and social sciences have been forced to retreat. This leads to a vital question. What is the ultimate value of a liberal arts education, such as provided by colleges like Indraprastha? For several centuries, now primarily in the west, people have devoted thought to the 'idea of the University' and have emphasized that scholarship in the humanities nurtures and preserves all that is humane in man's personality and civilization. In this millenium, when a single-minded devotion to information technology and business management seems to have nullified the value of the study of humanities, practitioners in the latter field continue to show their conscientious engagement with preservation of sane and civilized behaviour.

In a study such as this, concerned with mapping the development of educated Indian women as reflected in the mirror of a college in Delhi, these accounts should not be regarded as redundant or extraneous. If it is granted that education is not solely imparted by explication of textbooks or set topics, that utmost care is to be taken by the pedagogue to enrich every student with ideas and qualities, then seminars, theatre workshops, street play performances become important. How else can a vigorous life of the mind be inculcated? It is not necessary to inquire whether at any given time, all students entered fully into, for example, feminist activities. A college organizes activities hoping that even those who are not actively participating are gaining in some way. It may give an ordinary student some confidence to confront difficult situations in life.

In the life of a human being, to reach the age of 75 is to enter a period of resignation, of what is called *vanaprastha*. In the life of an institution, which has tenaciously survived through the vagaries of fortune, the passing of the same number of years gives courage and new hope to reinvent itself. Indraprastha College has encountered the indifference and hostility of society towards women's education, hostility of the colonial government towards a nationalist institution, suspicion directed against its secularist intentions, and periodic severe financial crises. It has triumphed over all to attain a mellow maturity.

NOTES AND REFERENCES

1. Nivedita Menon, 'Women and Citizenry', in Partha Chatterjee (ed.), *Wages of Freedom: Fifty Years of Indian Nation State*, Oxford University Press, New Delhi, 1998, p. 251.

2. Neerja Choudhury, 'Women in Politics: A Hop and a Skip but No Jump', in Shanta Serbjeet Singh and Jyoti Sabherwal (ed.), *A Feminine Critique*, Sterling Publishers Ltd., New Delhi, 1998, p. 29.

3. Tilottama Sharma, 'Influence of Mao's thoughts on Indian Students, 1966–71, Looking Back', in G. Phukan and D. Bhagwati (eds), *Mao Zedong and Social Reconstruction*, South Asia Publications, New Delhi, 1996, p. 151.

4. Ibid., p. 152.

5. Urvashi Butalia, 'Not the Happiest Years of My Life', in Uma Chakravarty, Radhika Singha, Ramya Sreenivasan (eds), *Reliving Miranda*, p. 129.

6. Akila Sivadas, 'Of Gheraos, Dharnas and Making a Difference', in Ibid., p. 123.

7. Geraldine Forbes, *Women in Modern India*, p. 224.

8. *The Hindustan Times*, March 11, 1979.

9. Ibid.

10. Radha Kumar, 'The Campaign Against Dowry', in Radha Kumar, *The History of Doing: An Illustrated Account of Movements for Women's Rights and Feminism in India*, Kali for Women, New Delhi, 1993, p. 119.

11. Manini Das, 'Women Against Dowry', in Madhu Kishwar and Ruth Vanita (ed.), *In Search of Answers: Indian Women's Voices from Manushi*, Zed Books Ltd., London, p. 222.

12. Amrita Chachchi, 'Media as a Political Statement', in Kamla Bhasin and Bina Aggarwal (eds), *Women in Media: Analysis, Alternatives and Action*, Kali for Women, New Delhi, 1984, p. 94.

13. Kumkum Sangari and Sudesh Vaid, *Women and Culture* (working paper No. 2), RCW, SNDT Women University, 1985, p. 1.

Bibliography

This bibliography contains only those select documents and books, which have either been used or have influenced the makings of this book.

PRIMARY SOURCES (UNPUBLISHED)

National Archives of India, New Delhi

Education and Health Wing

Education Branch: Proceedings, 1911–32 (selected)
Files, 1932–44 (selected)
Bureau of Education: On Macaulay's Minutes
Education of Girls in India (statistics),
October 1917

Legislative Department

Legislative Branch: Proceedings, 1917

Shri Narain Prasad's Haveli in Chandni Chowk, Delhi

Files, Correspondence, Souvenirs Relating to Indraprastha School

'The Education of Indian Girls', Speech of Annie Besant to The Theosophical Society in 1903
Quarterly Report of Indraprastha Hindu Kanya Shikshalaya ending 30 June, 1906
Half Yearly Reports of Indraprastha Hindu Kanya Shikshalaya, December 1906–December 1925
Revised Rules and Regulations of Indraprastha Hindu Kanya Shikshalaya, 1906
Matriculation Classes Endowment Fund, Indraprastha School, 1916

Prospectus of Indraprastha Hindu Girls High School and Intermediate College, May 1926

The Visitors Book, 1904–24

Smarika 1972

Indraprastha School Souvenirs, 1995 and 1997

Founder's Birth Centenary Souvenir, 1978

Files, Correspondence, Souvenirs Relating to Indraprastha College

Minutes of the College Managing Committee, 1924–32

Minutes of the College Governing Body, 1932–44

Minutes of the Board of Trustees, 1924–43

Indraprastha Educational Trust—Meetings and Agenda, 1970s–1980s

Correspondence Files, 1935–39; 1939–50 (Leonara G'meiner and Lala Jagdish Prasad)

Registration and Recognition as Degree College, Delhi University, October 1936–December 1940

Correspondence Files, August 1937–July 1943 (Kalavati Gupta)

Alipore House Files, February 1925–December 1937

Papers regarding lease of land, Copy of Minutes, June 1932–June 1941

Leonara G'meiner Memorial Fund File

Memorandum of Association and Rules and Regulations of Indraprastha Girls College, March 1932

Certificate of Registration under Societies Registration Act XXI of 1860, 30 January, 1953

Memorandum of Association of Indraprastha Educational Trust

Revision of College Society Rules, April 1936–August 1959

Papers regarding the Appointment of Principals

Hostel File

Registrar, Joint Stock Co., March 1932–January 1958

University of Delhi, Convocation Address, 1931 by Professor M. Abdur Rahman, Vice Chancellor

The Visitors Book, 1924 onwards

The Indraprastha Girls College, Delhi, A Retrospect, 1924–39 (printed in February 1939 to mark the inauguration of the college at Alipur House)

Student Handbook (Issued by Bina Das Gupta)

The Handbook of the Indian Section, The Theosophical Society, printed by The Theosophical Society, Varanasi

From Shri Brij Bans Kishore

Delhi University Calendar, 1934–37

All India Trade Directory and Who's Who, 1943

H.C. Bahadur (ed.), *The Kayastha*, Vol. XIII, Nos. 2–3, February–March 1946

'Rajshri Dr Ram Kishore', Smarika, Akhil Bhartiya Kayastha Mahasabha Shatabdi Samorah Samapan Parv, 26–27 December 1987

Minutes of the Meeting held on 30 October, 1993 at the residence of Justice R.S. Narula, Delhi Bar Association Centenary Celebrations, Vol. 1888–1993

Indraprastha College Library, Delhi

Lala Shri Ram, Remembering Lala Shri Ram: Reminiscences On His 100th Birthday

The Torch Bearer (hand written college magazine), May 1937

College Magazines—*Pradeep, Silhouette, Aaroh* (selected)

Principal's Annual Reports (selected)

Annual Report, Silver Jubilee, 1924–50

Annual Report, Golden Jubilee, 1924–74

Souvenir, Golden Jubilee, *The Golden Oriole*, 1924–74

Souvenir, Diamond Jubilee, 1924–84

St. Stephens College Library, Delhi

Aditya Bhattacharya, 'From An Ivory Tower', *The Stephanian*, Vol. LXXXVIII, No. 1, Winter 1978–79

Rev. S.A.C. Ghose, 'Forty Years' Recollections', St. Stephens College Magazine, Jubilee Supplement, December 1931

PUBLISHED SOURCES

Adam, William, *Reports on the State of Education in Bengal. 1835 & 1838*, edited by Ananthnath Basu, Reprinted, Government Publishing, Calcutta, 1941

Besant, Annie, *Speeches and Writings*, Nateson & Co., n.d., Madras

———, *Birth of New India: Collection of Writings and Speeches on Indian Affairs*, Theosophical Society, Madras, 1917

Dutt, S. (ed.), *The Delhi University Magazine*, Vol. 2, No. 1, April 1945

———, *The Delhi University Magazine*, Vol. 3, No. 1, April 1946

Leitner, G.W., *History of Indigenous Education in the Punjab Since Annexation and in 1882, 1883*, (first published 1883), Reprinted, Languages Department, Punjab, Patiala, 1973

Long, J., *Three Reports on the State of Education in Bengal and Bihar*, Government Publishing, Calcutta, 1868

Mill, John Stuart, *The Subjection of Women* (first published, D. Appleton Co., New York, 1869), Reprinted and edited by Edward Alexander, Transaction Publishers, New Brunswick, N.J., 2001

Richey, J.A., *Selections from Educational Records, 1920–22*, Reprinted, Calcutta, 1965

Sharp, H. (ed.), *Selections from Educational Records*, Part I, 1781–1839; Part II, 1840–59, Government Publishing, Calcutta, 1920

University Handbook 1995, Association of Indian Universities, 1995

NEWSPAPERS/MAGAZINES (SELECTED ISSUES)

Bombay Chronicle
Indian Express
Navbharat Times
New India
The Hindustan Times
The Leader
The National Call
The Patriot
The Pioneer
The Statesman
The Times of India
The Tribune
Chand, Allahabad, September 1929
Femina, May 10, 1974; December 1979–January 1980; August 8–22, 1984

INTERVIEW/CORRESPONDENCE/TALK BY FORMER STUDENTS/ TEACHERS OF INDRAPRASTHA COLLEGE

Shanti Nigam, student, 1934–38
Sarla Sharma, student, 1936–40
Monta Bose, student, 1931–33; lecturer, 1941–81
Prem Mukhi Saxena, student, 1935–39; lecturer, 1942–86
Nirmala Sherjung, lecturer, 1939–80
Kamla Mehta, student, 1939–43
Rup Seth, student, 1940–44
Qurratullain Haider, student, 1941–45
Pushpa Murgai, student, 1941–45
Vijay Mehrotra, student, 1941–47

MODERN WORKS

Amin, Sonia Nishat, *The World of Muslim Women in Colonial Bengal, 1876–1939*, E.J. Brill, Leiden, 1996

Asaf Ali, Aruna, *The Resurgence of Indian Women*, Radiant Publishers, New Delhi, 1991

Bali, Arun, P., *College Teachers: Challenges and Responses (A Case Study of Delhi University)*, Northern Book Centre, New Delhi, 1986

Basu, Aparna, *The Growth of Education and Political Development in India, 1898–1920*, Oxford University Press, New Delhi, 1974

———, *Essays in the History of Indian Education*, Concept Publishing House, New Delhi, 1982

———, 'The Foundation and Early History of Delhi University', R.E. Frykenberg (ed.), *Delhi Through the Ages: Essays in Urban History, Culture and Society*, Oxford University Press, New Delhi, 1988

———, 'Indian Higher Education: Colonialism and Beyond', Philip Altbach and V. Selvaratnam (ed.), *From Dependence to Autonomy: The Development of Asian Universities*, Kluwer Academic Publishers, London, 1989

——— (ed.), *University of Delhi, 1922–1997*, Platinum Jubilee, University of Delhi, 1998

Beggs, Tom, *The Excellent Women: The Origin and History of Queen Margaret College*, John Donald, Edinburgh, 1994

Bhattacharya, Sabyasachi (ed.), *The Contested Terrain: Perspectives on Education in India*, Orient Longman, New Delhi, 1998

——— (ed.), *Education and the Disprivileged: Nineteenth and Twentieth Century in India*, Orient Longman, New Delhi, 2002

———, Joseph Bara, Chinna Rao Yagati, B.M. Sankhdher (ed.), *The Development of Women's Education in India, 1850–1920*, Kanishka Publishers, New Delhi, 2001

———, Joseph Bara and Chinna Rao Yagati (ed.), *Educating the Nation: Documents on the Discourses of National Education in India, 1880–1920*, Kanishka Publishers, New Delhi, 2003

Burton, Antoinette, *Dwelling in the Archive: Women Writing House, Home, And History in Late Colonial India*, Oxford University Press, New Delhi, 2003

Chachchi, Amrita, 'Media As A Political Statement', Kamla Bhasin and Bina Aggarwal (ed.), *Women in Media: Analysis, Alternatives and Action*, Kali for Women, New Delhi, 1984

Chakrabarty, Sambuddha, *Antare Andare*, Stree, Calcutta, 1995

Chakravarti, Uma, *Rewriting History: The Life and Times of Pandita Ramabai*, Kali for Women in association with The Book Review Literary Trust, New Delhi, 1998

————, Radhika Singha, Ramya Sreenivasan (ed.), *Reliving Miranda, 1948-98*, College Publication, 1998

Chanana, Karuna (ed.), *Socialization, Education and Women: Exploration of Gender Identity*, Orient Longman, New Delhi, 1988

Chatterjee, Partha, 'The Nation and its Women', Ranajit Guha (ed.), *A Subaltern Studies Reader, 1986–1995*, Oxford University Press, New Delhi, 1998

Chaudhuri, Nirad, C., *The Autobiography of An Unknown Indian*, California University Press, Berkeley, 1968

Choudhury, Neerja, 'Women in Politics: A Hop and A Skip but No Jump', Shanta Serbjeet Singh and Jyoti Sabherwal (ed.), *A Feminine Critique*, Sterling Publishers Ltd., New Delhi, 1998

Das, Manini, 'Women Against Dowry', Madhu Kishwar and Ruth Vanita (ed.), *In Search of Answers: Indian Women's Voices from Manushi*, Zed Books Ltd., London, 1984

Dhar, Sheila, *Here's Someone I'd Like You To Meet*, Oxford University Press, New Delhi, 1995

Dharampal, *The Beautiful Tree: Indigenous Education in the Eighteenth Century*, Biblia Impex Private Ltd., New Delhi, 1983

Forbes, Geraldine, *Women in Modern India*, The New Cambridge History of India, IV.2, Cambridge University Press, Cambridge, 1996

Ghosh, Suresh Chandra, *The History of Education in Modern India, 1757–1998*, (first published, Orient Longman, New Delhi, 1995), Revised edition, Orient Longman, New Delhi, 2000

Gupta, Narayani, *Delhi Between Two Empires, 1803–1931*, Oxford University Press, New Delhi, 1981

———— and Sheila Uttam Singh, 'The Interior And The Exterior: Indraprastha College For Women', Mushirul Hasan (ed.), *Knowledge, Power and Politics: Educational Institutions in India*, Lotus Collection, Roli Books, New Delhi, 1998

Hasan, Mushirul (ed.), *Knowledge, Power and Politics: Educational Institutions in India*, Lotus Collection, Roli Books, New Delhi, 1998

Hossain, Rokeya Sakhawat, 'Abarodhbasini', Abdul Qadir (ed.), *Rokeya Rachanabali*, Bangla Academy, Dacca, 1984

Ikramullah, Shaista Suhrawardy, *From Purdah to Parliament*, (first published Csesset Press, London, 1963), Oxford India Paperback, New Delhi, 2000

Jayawardene, Kumari, *Feminism and Nationalism in the Third World*, Kali for Women, New Delhi, 1986

Kamath, Shanti and Narain Prasad, *The Saga of Indraprastha College For Women*, Indraprastha Educational Trust, Platinum Jubilee, Delhi, 1999

Karve, D.K., *Looking Back*, Hindu Widows Home Association, Poona, 1931

Keer, Dhananjay, *Jotirao Phooley: Father of the Indian Social Revolution*, Popular Prakashan, Bombay, 1964

Kumar, Krishna, *Political Agenda of Education: A Study of Colonialist and Nationalist Ideas*, Sage Publications, New Delhi, 1991

————, 'Colonial Citizen, an Educational Ideal', mimeograph and microfilm, Nehru Memorial Museum and Library, New Delhi

Kumar, Radha, *The History of Doing: An Illustrated Account of Movements for Women's Rights and Feminism in India, 1800–1990*, Kali for Women, New Delhi, 1993

Lateef, Shahida, *Muslim Women in India: Political and Private Realities*, Kali for Women, New Delhi, 1990

Mannheim, Karl and W.C. Stewart, *An Introduction to the Sociology of Education*, Routledge & Kegan Paul, London, 1962

Maskiell, Michelle, *Women Between Cultures: The Lives of Kinnaird College Alumnae in British India*, Syracuse University, USA, 1984

Mehta, Rama, *The Western Educated Hindu Women*, Asia Publishing House, Bombay, 1970

Menon, Nivedita, 'Women and Citizenry', Partha Chatterjee (ed.), *Wages of Freedom: Fifty Years of Indian Nation State*, Oxford University Press, New Delhi, 1998

Menon, Ritu and Kamla Bhasin, 'Recovery, Rupture, Resistance: Indian State and Abduction of Women During Partition', *Economic and Political Weekly*, Vol. 28, No. 17, April 1993

Minault, Gail, *Secluded Scholars: Women's Education and Moral Social Reform in Colonial India*, (Gender Studies Series), Oxford University Press, New Delhi, 1998

————, *Voices of Silence*, English translation of Khwaja Altaf Hussain Hali's *Majalis Un–Nissa* and *Chup Ki Dad*, Chanakya, New Delhi, 1986

————, 'Other Voices, Other Rooms: The View from the *Zenana*', Nita Kumar (ed.), *Women as Subjects: South Asian Histories*, University Press of Virginia, Charlottesville, 1994

Monk, F.F., *A History of St. Stephens College, Delhi* (compiled for the Cambridge Mission for the 50th anniversary in 1931), YMCA Publishing House, Calcutta, 1935

Nanda, B.R. (ed.), *Indian Women: From Purdah to Modernity*, Vikas Publishing House, New Delhi, 1996

Nath, Asha, *Educating the Indian Women: The Story of Sharda Divan*, Radiant Publishers, New Delhi, 1992

Nehru, Jawaharlal, *The Discovery of India*, New Delhi, 1964

Ray, Bharati, *Early Feminists of Colonial India: Sarala Devi*

Chaudhurani & Rokeya Sakhawat Hossain, Oxford University Press, New Delhi, 2002

────── (ed.), *From the Seams of History: Essays on Indian Women*, Reprint, Oxford University Press, New Delhi, 2001

Sangari, Kumkum, *Politics of the Possible: Essays on Gender History, Narratives, Colonial English*, Tulika (Paperback), New Delhi, 2001

────── and Sudesh Vaid (ed.), *Recasting Women: Essays in Colonial History*, Kali for Women, New Delhi, 1989

────── and Sudesh Vaid, *Women and Culture*, SNDT Women's University, Bombay, 1985

Sarkar, Sumit, *Modern India, 1885–1947*, Macmillan, New Delhi, 1983

Sharma, Sarla, 'Sangeet Roopak, 1929–47', (unpublished)

Sharma, S. Ram, *Women and Education*, 3 vols., Discovery Publishing House, New Delhi, 1995

Sharma, Sunaina and Madhu Kishwar, 'Toofani Satyawati: An Unsung Hero of Freedom Struggle', *Manushi*, No. 107, July–August 1998

Sharma, Tilottama, 'Influence of Mao's Thoughts on Indian Students, 1966–71, Looking Back', G. Phukan and D. Bhagwati (ed.), *Mao Zedong and Social Reconstruction*, South Asia Publications, New Delhi, 1996

Siddiqui, Mujibul Hasan, *Women Education: A Research Approach*, APH Publishers, New Delhi, 1993

Swaminathan, Padmini, 'Women's Education in Colonial Tamilnadu, 1900–30: The Coalescence of Patriarchy and Colonialism', *Indian Journal of Gender Studies*, Vol. VI, No. 2, July–December 1999

Index